THE MENTAL TOUGHNESS HANDBOOK 2022

A STEP-BY-STEP GUIDE TO FACING LIFE
AND OVERCOME ADVERSITIES WITH COURAGE AND
EQUILIBRIUM!

CONTENTS

Introduction
I. Fundamentals of Mental Toughness

    What Is Mental Toughness (And How Does It Differ from Grit)?
    10 Benefits of Becoming Mentally Tough
    Top 7 Traits of Mentally Tough People
    8 Sworn Enemies of Mental Toughness

II. Pivotal Factors in Developing Mental Toughness
    Mental Toughness and Emotional Mastery
    Mental Toughness and Mental Resilience
    Mental Toughness in the Face of Adversity
    Mental Toughness and the Importance of Delaying Gratification
    Mental Toughness and Your Habits
    Talent, Ability, and Confidence: How They Influence Mental Toughness
    How Your Attitude Affects Your Mental Toughness
    Mental Toughness and Your Inner Critic
    The Role of Willpower and Motivation
    The Role of Self-Discipline
    How to Reject the Desire to Give Up
    The Upside of Boredom
    How to Learn the RIGHT Lessons from Failure
    How Navy SEALs Develop Mental Toughness

III. A Quick-Start Guide to Becoming Mentally Tough
    Practical Applications of Mental Toughness
    A 10-Step Training Program for Toughening Your Mind
    The Mental Toughness Maintenance Guide

Final Thoughts On Developing Mental Toughness
Did You Enjoy Reading The Mental Toughness Handbook?

INTRODUCTION

~

Anyone who has achieved lasting success possesses mental toughness. Athletes, corporate executives, teachers, parents, students, entrepreneurs, authors… the field of expertise is irrelevant. The fact that an individual has excelled over the long run is sufficient evidence that he or she is mentally tough.

There's no other way to attain persistent excellence. The road to enduring success is paved with obstacles.

No one is spared the gauntlet.

Mental toughness is required to overcome hurdles that threaten to derail us from our goals. This state of mind can literally mean the difference between success and failure.

The Many Names of Mental Toughness

A lot of terms are used synonymously with mental toughness, and some are less accurate than others. Following are examples:

- grit
- persistance
- tenacity
- perseverance
- stoicism
- resilience
- resoluteness
- resolve
- mental stamina
- mental fortitude
- discipline

We'll distinguish the finer details in *Part I: Fundamentals of Mental Toughness*. For now, it's enough to understand the general principle: mental toughness is our durability in the face of adversity.

You'll see this principle illustrated in greater detail as we examine the many facets of personal durability and resolve in *Part II: Pivotal Factors in Developing Mental Toughness*. We'll cover a lot of material in *Part II*. This section of the book moves quickly and includes plenty of exercises to help you apply what you've learned.

Lastly, in *Part III: A Quick-Start Guide to Becoming Mentally Tough*, we'll go through a 10-step program for building you resilience from the ground up. You'll also learn how to maintain your newly-developed mental toughness throughout your life.

What This Book Is (And Is NOT) About

The goal of this book is to help you achieve greater levels of success in whatever area of your life you'd like to focus on. In short, I'm going to show you how to build mental resilience and overcome any obstacle, setback, or misfortune life throws at you.

It's going to take more than optimistic platitudes and positive self-talk. I won't lie to you; it's going to entail hard work. It'll take effort, and there'll be plenty of frustration along the way. But the rewards for becoming mentally tough are considerable. You'll feel more effectual, powerful, and influential. You'll feel as if you can achieve anything you set your mind to.

The confidence you'll build from this gradual change in mindset - and it *is* a gradual process - will help you to literally transform your life. Whether that means excelling as a parent, enjoying greater success as a business owner, or improving the relationships you enjoy with your friends and loved ones depends on your focus.

In my opinion, most personal development books are too long. They're filled with anecdotes, cheerleading, and research-driven prose that borders on intellectual grandstanding.

This book is different. It's light on the above and heavy on *actionable* advice, stuff you can start using today. My goal is to cover the requisite material thoroughly but quickly so you can apply the advice as soon as possible. Nothing would make me happier than for you to read this short book and take purposeful, immediate action based on its instruction.

How to Make This Book Work for YOU

You'll come across numerous exercises throughout the book. Please don't ignore them. Take the time to complete them. Most of the exercises are very simple, and require little time and effort.

I suspect many readers will gloss over them for those reasons alone, dismissing them because they're easy and quick. I encourage you to be different. Do the exercises with confidence that they'll help you to become mentally tough. While this book isn't technically a workbook, it *does* prioritize taking action over mere learning.

Why? Because *applying* the information you learn is necessary if you hope to use it to change your life.

We know this from experience. I've lost count of the number of books I've read and workshops I've attended where the guidance was lost on me due to my failure to put the information to use. Perhaps you can relate to that mistake.

So again, please do the exercises. You'll be happy you did by the time you finish reading this book.

Your Mission, If You Choose to Accept It…

Has success been fleeting in your life? Have you had difficulty achieving and maintaining greatness in your chosen areas of focus? Has life thrown you unexpected curve balls that have left you feeling discouraged, angry, and depressed?

If so, today is the perfect day to start making positive changes.

No matter where you are in your life, no matter what struggles you're currently experiencing, you can improve your circumstances. You can achieve greater levels of success. This fact should fill you with practical optimism. After all, you have tremendous influence over your mindset. Control *that*, and the battle is nearly won.

The Mental Toughness Handbook will prepare you for the fight. It'll give you the necessary tools, offer a methodical game plan, and provide the training you'll need to become increasingly durable in the face of adversity.

We'll be going on this journey together. I'll be your tour guide, and will ensure you maximize your time and attentional resources. By the time we're done, assuming you do the exercises, you'll notice your mindset has already begun to change.

You'll have started to truly become mentally tough.

Does that sound good to you? Then let's jump in.

PART I

FUNDAMENTALS OF MENTAL TOUGHNESS

∽

No one is born with mental toughness. We develop it over time, similar to building a muscle. That's wonderful news because it means anyone can do it. All that is required is commitment.

The reason so many *don't* develop mental toughness is because it entails a lot of work and patience, and comes with a fair bit of frustration. It involves discomfort. You're part of a special group because you're willing to put in the work and endure the frustration to develop a state of mind that'll reward you throughout your life.

But first things first. Before you can develop mental toughness, it's important to understand its many facets. That's what we'll focus on in this section. We'll examine what mental toughness is and how it'll improve your life. I'll also describe the telltale traits of people who have mastered it. You'll be able to use this as a checklist for personal comparison as you develop the skill yourself.

Finally, we'll highlight several enemies of mental toughness. These are the obstacles that'll try to discourage you from persevering when circumstances fail to go your way. After you finish reading Part I, you'll be acutely aware of these obstacles. This advance awareness will help you to overcome them when you confront them.

One quick note: you've probably glanced at this book's table of contents. If so, you've noticed there are a lot of chapters. Don't feel daunted. Most of the chapters are short because we'll be focusing on *applying the material.*

Minimal theory, maximum action.

Onward.

WHAT IS MENTAL TOUGHNESS (AND HOW DOES IT DIFFER FROM GRIT)?

I provided a simple definition earlier: mental toughness is durability in the face of adversity. But there's a lot going on in that definition, so let's unpack it.

First, it involves our reaction to stress. Do we crumble or persist? Do we give up or stay the course?

Second, it involves our responses to our emotions. What do we do when we feel frustrated? How do we deal with our anger and disappointment when life seems unfair to us?

Third, it involves our resilience. When things go wrong in our lives, do we dust ourselves off and get back on track or complain and blame others for our predicaments?

Fourth, it involves our grit. When we face roadblocks to achieving our goals, do we press onward or concede defeat?

Grit and mental toughness are often considered to be the same thing. In truth, they're not. Grit is an attribute that defines our inclination to persevere in adverse circumstances. Mental toughness is a *state of mind*. It defines our attitudinal *durability* in such circumstances. It describes our general outlook.

In that way, it's closer to stoicism than grit.

Having said that, grit is a crucial ingredient in developing mental toughness. Grit helps us to regulate our responses to our negative emotions. It fills us with the confidence we need to focus on achievement rather than our fear of failure. It's impossible to be mentally tough and not possess a healthy amount of grit.

Now that we've unpacked the definition of mental toughness, let's flesh it out with a few real-life examples.

Real-Life Examples of Mental Toughness

You probably know at least one athlete. If this person cares about his or her performance, he or she possesses mental toughness. Athletes, from football players to figure skaters, put their minds and bodies through the wringer. There's no way they can endure the punishing discipline required of them and the disappointment that accompanies performing below their standards without developing a level of mental durability.

You probably also know at least one entrepreneur. If that person has built a successful business, you can be sure he or she has experienced times of extreme stress. Entrepreneurs and business owners face countless obstacles and setbacks. The only way they can succeed in the long run is to endure and overcome them.

Consider doctors and nurses. These professionals deal with life-and-death situations every day, and none of these situations are scripted. Whether in the emergency room or the operating room, things often go wrong. Unanticipated complications surface at the worst possible times. The only way doctors and nurses can perform effectively is by regulating their emotions, accepting their current circumstances, and acting quickly when things go awry.

Consider first responders, those who are tasked with arriving at the scene of an emergency and providing specialized help. They include firemen, police officers, paramedics, and other highly-trained individuals. They work in extremely stressful environments. They're expected to perform at a high level, often when their lives are at risk. There's no way they can do so without possessing mental toughness.

If you're a parent, you undoubtedly have a healthy measure of mental toughness already, even if it is focused in a single area of your life. Raising children involves uncertainty and fear. Unforeseen trauma - for example, an injury or serious illness - must be addressed in the face of panic and negative emotions. Immediate happiness must often be sacrificed for future rewards. Raising healthy, confident, capable, self-sufficient children requires weathering times of stress, fear, and guilt.

Becoming Mentally Strong in Every Area of Your Life

The above are examples of mental toughness exhibited by people you probably know. In fact, you may *be* one of these people. But mental toughness exhibited in one area of our lives often eludes us in other areas.

For example, my ability to endure adverse situations while running my business doesn't mean I'd be able to endure the challenges that accompany raising a child. Likewise, a doctor who's able to remain calm and effective in the emergency room may be unable to endure the gnawing stress that accompanies marital problems.

This book will show you how to become mentally strong in *all* areas of your life. Once you become so, you'll enjoy the peace of mind that comes with knowing you can handle any situation with poise, grace, and self-confidence.

10 BENEFITS OF BECOMING MENTALLY TOUGH

∼

As we noted earlier, developing mental toughness requires work and patience, and is accompanied by frustration. The only reason to put yourself through this experience is the expectation that doing so will noticeably improve your life. To that end, let's quickly examine 10 ways that toughening your mind against adversity will benefit you for years to come.

Benefit #1 - Greater Resistance to Negative Emotions

Emotions are a double-edged sword. On the one hand, they allow us to experience joy, motivate us to take action, and help us to empathize with others. However, they can also sabotage us. Negative emotions, such as anger, shame, fear, and anxiety prompt us to make terrible decisions, hide mistakes, and feel like giving up when things go awry.

When you become mentally tough, you'll be better able to regulate your emotions. You'll still be in touch with them, but *negative* feelings will have less impact on your behavior and responses to adverse conditions.

Benefit #2 - Improved Performance

Peak performance stems from your mindset. This includes how you respond to setbacks. Whether you're an athlete, surgeon, chef, or musician, your ability to perform at a high level depends on how you feel and react when things go wrong. If you wilt when you encounter setbacks, your performance will suffer. Worse, you'll never fully reach your potential.

Mental toughness prepares you for obstacles. Rather than wilting when you encounter them, you'll approach them with grace and self-confidence. You'll be better able to weather difficult or unplanned circumstances and overcome challenges.

Benefit #3 - Confidence That Circumstances Will Improve

If you're not resilient to adversity, it's easy to become fatalistic when things go wrong. You may feel like giving up, convinced that life isn't fair. You might be inclined to concede defeat, telling yourself that persevering would be for naught because current conditions are unlikely to get better.

But that's a false assumption. Circumstances always change. And they often do so as a result of our actions. Stressful situations can either become more stressful or relaxing based on our behavioral responses to stress-inducing stimuli. Uncomfortable situations can either become more uncomfortable or pleasant based on how we react to our environments.

When you're mentally resilient to difficult situations, you're able to tolerate them, confident that your resolve will be rewarded as circumstances inevitably improve.

Benefit #4 - Greater Ability to Manage Stress

Stress stems from the expectation of consequences, both real and perceived. It comes from the knowledge that high stakes are involved in whatever we're doing. If we perform poorly, something bad will happen.

For example, salespeople must hit their sales quotas or risk losing their jobs and income. Firefighters must perform their jobs effectively or others might lose their lives. Athletes must perform at a high level or risk being outperformed by their competitors.

Mental strength allows you to endure the pressure. Rather than succumbing to it, you're able to thrive under it. Your tenacity helps you to stay motivated, optimistic, and confident in your abilities in high-stress situations.

Benefit #5 - Less Susceptibility to Self-Doubt

No one escapes self-doubt entirely. Show me someone who always *seems* self-possessed, even to the point of arrogance, and I'll show you someone who occasionally (and perhaps even frequently) second-guesses himself or herself.

Self-doubt affects us all. We wonder whether we'll be able to compete effectively. We question whether we'll achieve our goals. We even entertain worst-case scenarios, allowing our inner critics to wreak havoc with our confidence.

Mental toughness doesn't eliminate self-doubt. Instead, it prevents self-doubt from sabotaging your performance. It gives you a chance to acknowledge that even though failure is a possibility, fear of it stems from insecurity rather than hard evidence. Success is probably more likely than your inner critic insinuates.

Benefit #6 - Greater Clarity Regarding Your Intentions and Purpose

Dealing with adverse situations is difficult when you're uncertain of the reasons you're doing so. It's hard to stay motivated to act if you're unclear about *why* you're putting in the effort.

For example, suppose you've spent months looking for a job. Leads are showing little promise and your savings account is dwindling dangerously low. It's easy to become frustrated. It's tempting to give up. Such is the power of despair because it focuses on failure, obfuscating your purpose in the process.

When you're mentally strong, you're able to focus on the reasons you're trying to accomplish your goal. You're less susceptible to feelings of hopelessness because you know *why* you're taking action. That knowledge keeps you motivated to face any challenges that come your way.

Benefit #7 - Fearlessness

Fear of the unknown is one of the most common obstacles to our achieving our potential. It manifests in different ways, but one of these ways is familiar to us all: alarm at the prospect of venturing beyond our comfort zones.

Humans place enormous value on comfort and predictability. We might claim to relish surprises and spontaneity, but in truth, most of us are creatures of habit. We follow routines. These routines make us feel comfortable and in control of our environments. To that end, the idea of trying something new causes us to hesitate. We fear the unknown.

Mental toughness erodes this fear. It gives us the courage to venture outside our comfort zones and try new things. To that end, it gives us the opportunity to grow, developing new skills and acquiring new knowledge and insight.

Benefit #8 - Ability to Accept (And Learn From) Failure

Failure is an inescapable part of life. It's an ever-present possibility whenever we try to accomplish something.

Most people will go to great lengths to avoid failure. They perceive it as an indictment of their character and value. Accordingly, they avoid taking risks and making mistakes, even though doing so stunts their personal and professional growth. Failure, to them, is unacceptable.

Mental resilience prepares you to not only accept failure as a potential outcome of any endeavor, but allows you to learn from your mistakes. Rather than perceiving failure as a judgement on your character and value, you'll see it as a chance to take corrective action for improved performance in the future. The prospect of failing will no longer hold any power over you.

Benefit #9 - Greater Ability to Delay Gratification

Given a choice, we prefer to experience gratification now rather than later. It's human nature. The problem is, this intuitive inclination often imposes negative consequences.

It motivates us to give up on our goals because they require too much effort. It chips away at our patience and impulse control as we perceive forbearance to be a type of needless suffering. It discourages us from working hard toward accomplishing an objective because we're tempted by the pleasures available to us in the moment.

Mental strength amplifies your ability to delay gratification. You'll no longer be at the mercy of your impulses. You'll be able to resist the temptations that surround you and devote your energy and attention to endeavors that promise bigger dividends down the road.

Benefit #10 - Willingness to Let Things Go

We tend to hold onto things that have caused us emotional pain. Examples include mistakes that carried terrible consequences, perceived slights from others, and regrettable decisions from our distant past. These things can sometimes begin to define us. They become a part of our identity. When they become so, they rob us of the inner peace and confidence we would otherwise experience.

When you develop mental toughness, you'll become more inclined to let such things go. Rather than dwelling on past pains and regrets, you'll see them as stepping stones to your continual growth. Every mistake become a lesson from which to acquire insight. Every perceived slight becomes an opportunity to nurture valued relationships. Every regrettable decision becomes a chance to reexamine your intentions and ensure they align with your values.

Ultimately, after these things have served their purpose, you'll be able to move on, leaving them where they belong: in the past.

THIS SECTION WAS A LONG ONE. But it's important to recognize what you stand to gain from pursuing mental toughness. Let's now investigate the common attributes of mentally-tough people.

TOP 7 TRAITS OF MENTALLY TOUGH PEOPLE

∼

Think of the people in your life who epitomize your definition of success. Maybe it's a family member who built a huge business in a competitive market. Maybe it's a friend who consistently accomplishes every personal and professional goal he sets for himself. Perhaps it's a coworker who's exceptionally effective at her job.

Like everyone, these individuals face adversity. Things go wrong during the course of their days. Unanticipated circumstances constantly threaten to derail them. Failure looms around each corner, and is sometimes unavoidable.

Yet they manage to persevere, ultimately succeeding in spite of these obstacles.

Each of these individuals has developed mental toughness. They've learned to be resilient when confronted with adverse situations. They're able to face challenges with grit, tenacity, and courage, confident in their abilities and assured by the fact that hardship and failure are inevitable.

It's worth placing these people under the microscope to learn what makes them tick. To that end, here are seven crucial attributes that comprise their mental toughness.

Trait #1: Ability to Disentangle Themselves from Things They Can't Influence

Like all of us, people who are mentally tough are passionate about a variety of things. For example, some tune into the latest political news, reading opinions and listening to pundits hoping to gain insight. For others, major issues like global warming, human trafficking, and food security attract their attention.

What sets apart mentally tough people is their quick recognition that, despite their interest, they're unable to influence most of these issues. This private concession allows them to disengage after doing what's possible, giving them the freedom to focus on things upon which they can have a significant impact.

Take global warming as an example. Individually, we can vote, we can sign petitions, and we can minimize our personal carbon footprint. But we lack the ability to materially influence the issue on a global scale. Spending countless hours trying to advance the matter without any hope for a justified and rewarding outcome is a recipe for despair.

Mentally tough people know when to disentangle themselves and move on.

Trait #2: Flexibility in Handling Unanticipated Events

Life throws curve balls. The moment we're confident that a situation will work out exactly as we anticipate, we encounter unforeseen circumstances that threaten to make a mess out of things.

Most people are surprised, and even paralyzed, by unexpected developments. This is another area in which mentally strong people stand apart from the pack. They realize that while making plans is useful, unpredicted situations can quickly ruin even the most carefully prepared plans. So they learn to adapt. They train themselves to be mentally flexible so they're able to adjust whenever they're confronted by unexpected circumstances.

Have you ever watched someone you know to be consistently successful in their pursuits? Have you ever wondered how they can remain calm when they encounter one obstacle after another? It's largely because of their adaptability, their psychological preparedness for the unexpected.

This is a key attribute among people who are mentally tough.

Trait #3: Strong Self-Awareness

Self-awareness is the recognition of your emotional state, the motives driving your decisions and actions, and the influence of your personality and temperament. That's a loose definition, but it'll suffice for now.

Mentally strong people are hyper self-aware. They have to be so. Their confidence to perform effectively and handle any situation that unfolds before them stems from this awareness. They trust themselves to adapt to changing circumstances and overcome obstacles not merely because of their strengths, but also because they acknowledge their weaknesses. This allows them to control their emotions, absorb stress, and remain resilient when things go awry.

Most people believe they possess strong self-awareness. But in my opinion, few actually do. Sure, most of us recognize things that trigger our emotions. We know certain triggers make us angry, tense, or happy. We're also aware that we harbor both good and bad traits. But *true* self-awareness extends much deeper. Mentally tough people achieve it by purposefully investigating their psyches and developing compensatory strategies that help them deal with adversity.

Trait #4: Willingness to Face Uncertain Circumstances

We talked about how mentally strong people possess the ability to adapt to unexpected events (Trait #2). They're also willing to face uncertainty. They recognize that none of their plans are foolproof. On the contrary, they intuitively know that all plans are susceptible to failure based on unanticipated events. As Helmuth von Moltke the Elder, Chief of Staff of the Prussian army in the 1800s said, "No battle plan survives contact with the enemy."

And despite this acknowledgement, they're inclined to press forward. They're ready to act knowing that potential failure looms around every corner.

This is an unusual attribute. Few of us are born with it. Rather, it's developed over time, usually by running a gauntlet of unfavorable situations that pose a continual threat of emotional, psychological, and even physical defeat. Show me a mentally tough person and I'll show you an individual who has successfully endured a long string of troubles and challenges.

Trait #5: Ability to Bounce Back from Disappointments

Life is full of disappointments. Some are small and have a negligible impact on our day. Others are weighty and can dominate our mind space for weeks on end. For example, suppose you've toiled at your job for years expecting to earn a promotion only to be overlooked when the time finally arrived. Or imagine training for years as an Olympic hopeful only to have your dreams dashed when you fail to qualify.

These types of disappointments can be so traumatic that they cause us to avoid taking risks in the future. They can make us apprehensive to the point that we're paralyzed, unable to set goals, make plans, and take action. In short, we'll go to great lengths to avoid experiencing such disappointments down the road.

Mentally strong people have a different perspective. Like all of us, they acknowledge that disappointments, big and small, are inevitable. But they also recognize that such occurrences can be terrific learning opportunities. And they investigate accordingly. Disappointing results often reveal tactics that aren't working, approaches that are ineffective, and mistakes that can be avoided henceforth.

This healthy perspective makes it easier for mentally tough individuals to bounce back when they fail.

Trait #6: Emotional Mastery

All of us experience negative emotions. They arise from disappointment, unmet expectations, and unforeseen events that complicate our lives.

For example, you may have felt disheartened after receiving a poor performance review at your job. Perhaps you felt angry at yourself when you received a terrible grade on an exam after spending several days preparing for it. Maybe you experienced profound frustration the last time unanticipated traffic on the freeway made you late for an important appointment.

Many of us live at the mercy of our emotions. That's a problem when we experience *negative* emotions, such as discouragement, anger, and frustration. These feelings hold us back. They prevent us from making rational decisions and taking productive action, and thereby hamper our personal and professional growth.

Mentally strong people have mastered their emotions. Their emotional intelligence (EQ) is higher than that of most of their peers. That's not to suggest they never experience negative emotions. Rather, it indicates they're aware of these feelings, are able to regulate themselves in light of them, and can move forward with purpose.

Trait #7: Practical Optimism

It's easy to become mired in the negativity that surrounds us. We're bombarded by it every day. Whether it's the latest political scandal or reports of a pending recession on the horizon, we can forgive ourselves for feeling gloomy and pessimistic.

Having said that, mental toughness is usually found in those who have a positive attitude. These individuals are optimistic about the future. To clarify, they're not the ebullient type who remain cheerful as their world crumbles. Rather, they're cautiously optimistic, seeing opportunities where others see only disaster and hopelessness. Mentally strong people are upbeat pragmatists. They protect their minds from negativity, refusing to dwell in it. Meanwhile, they remain confident in their abilities and sound judgment to make the best of every situation.

The Good News about Mental Toughness

No one is born mentally strong. It's something each of us develops. That's terrific news because it means that you control it. You can incorporate each of the seven traits profiled above into your life. Rather than being paralyzed with fear, frustration, and lack of confidence when things go wrong, you can develop the mental resilience you need to perform effectively.

Now that we've covered the most common attributes of mentally strong individuals, let's switch gears. Let's take a look at some of the biggest obstacles you'll encounter on the road to developing mental toughness.

8 SWORN ENEMIES OF MENTAL TOUGHNESS

~

Learning to face complications and setbacks while remaining confident in your ability to persevere is a long road. If developing mental resiliency were easy, everyone would do it and the idea of giving up would be strange to us. The fact is, life throws obstacles in our path that can seem, in the moment, overwhelming. We must train our minds to withstand the despair and hopelessness that chip away at our confidence and optimism when things go awry.

There are several adversaries you'll meet along the way. In fact, you may already be acquainted with some of them. Each one will try to intimidate you and pressure you to surrender when situations become difficult to handle.

Below, we'll take a look at the eight most common threats to your burgeoning psychological tenacity. By the end of this section, you'll know exactly which hazards to look for as you gradually strengthen your resolve. If you can identify them before they rear their heads, you'll be better equipped to overcome them.

Enemy #1: Self-Pity

Feeling sorry for ourselves is exhausting. It takes a lot of energy. It also sabotages our resolve, making us more likely to resign ourselves to failure than persevere through difficult situations. We end up dwelling on our unfavorable circumstances rather than toughening our minds to see our way through them.

That affects our behavior. Instead of rolling up our sleeves and digging our heels in, we focus on the fact that everything is going wrong. We wallow in that negativity, which prevents us from taking the necessary action to overcome our adverse conditions.

Such is the danger inherent in self-pity. It is the bane of psychological resilience.

Enemy #2: Self-Doubt

It's difficult to stay mentally strong in unfavorable situations when you lack confidence in your abilities and skills. But lack of ability and skill is rarely the main factor that determines whether you'll fail or overcome your circumstances. The deciding factor is usually insecurity. Insecurity breeds inaction, which is a much larger threat to your success.

There's nothing wrong with feeling self-doubt. Doing so is natural. It's our brain's way of both protecting us and preparing us for the hard work ahead. Fortune 500 CEOs, world-class athletes, top film directors, and even presidents experience it.

The trouble begins when we allow self-doubt to possess such a foothold in our minds that it paralyzes us. All of our energy becomes focused on our perceived deficits that our insecurity incapacitates us.

Enemy #3: Your Inner Critic

This enemy is related to Enemy #2 above. But it deserves its own spotlight because it can have such a crippling effect on our cognitive resolve.

Each of us has an inner critic. It's the voice in our heads telling us that we're not good enough, smart enough, or attractive enough. It's the nag that tries to convince us that we don't deserve the success we seek. It finds fault in everything we do, and asserts that others will do the same.

Your inner critic may prove to be your most challenging adversary as you develop mental toughness. It will not only dwell on the negative aspects of your performance (both perceived and real), but it'll try to get you to do the same. And once your mind is focused on negativity, your inner critic will have successfully distracted you from strengthening your resolve.

Becoming mentally strong requires silencing negative self-talk. In *Part II: Pivotal Factors In Developing Mental Toughness*, I'll share some tips for showing your inner critic who's the boss.

Enemy #4: Fear

Fear comes in a lot of flavors. We fear disappointing others. We fear not meeting their expectations. We fear not meeting our *own* expectations. We fear failure. We fear success. We fear the unfamiliar and unknown.

Regardless of its form, fear sabotages our psychological resilience. It erodes our resolve, releases unhealthy emotions, and causes us to focus on potentially negative outcomes. We freeze up, overwhelmed by the possibility of disaster.

Fear distorts reality. It implies that catastrophe and ruination are certain to follow our performance. If we allow fear to gain a foothold in our minds, we end up feeling defeated before we've even taken action. The truth is, the odds of catastrophe resulting from whatever we're doing are so infinitesimal that they're unworthy of consideration.

Fear takes every potentially negative outcome and amplifies its impact. For example, if we're about to give a presentation, our fear may tell us that we'll be ridiculed by our audience and forever branded an incompetent failure. In reality, we're likely to leave a favorable impression on our audience even if a few things fail to go as planned.

Fear is an emotion that opposes the development of mental toughness. Once the latter develops, fear is rendered powerless.

Enemy #5: Laziness

There's nothing wrong with feeling lazy. Nor is there anything wrong with taking the opportunity to relax. We must do so on a regular basis. The alternative is burnout. And burnout is a much greater threat to your performance and productivity than bouts of laziness. Having said that, laziness can breed *additional* laziness if it's left unchecked.

For example, suppose your alarm goes off in the morning and rather than immediately getting out of bed you hit the snooze button. After a few minutes, you hit it again. And then again. By the time you finally get out of bed, you're feeling sluggish. And you're running late, to boot. Your morning is off to an idle start, and that sets the tone for your performance later in the day.

In this case, early laziness opened the door to a general sense of lethargy. And this feeling of sluggishness will make you less likely to persevere when things go wrong. Rather than digging in and persisting through adversity, your mental torpor will encourage you to concede defeat.

Enemy #6: Perfectionism

All of us want to perform without fault. At work, we'd like to give flawless presentations. At home, we'd like our living spaces to be completely free of clutter. While participating in sports, we'd like to display impeccable execution. In school, we'd like to ace every assignment and exam.

In short, we'd prefer to be perfect.

Most of us are willing to admit that we're *not* perfect. But for some of us, the idea of being less than perfect is anathema to our sensibilities. We're unable to accept it. So we struggle to be perfect in everything we do, partly to satisfy our own expectations and partly to avoid disappointing *others'* expectations.

The problem is, perfectionism is the scourge of mental toughness. Nothing breeds inaction and erodes cognitive resilience as completely as the nagging thought that any performance that's less than perfect is unacceptable. This self-harassment breeds self-doubt and gives center stage to your inner critic.

Enemy #7: Emotionalism

Our emotions can be our best ally or our worst adversary. Sometimes, we experience joy, hope, love, and inspiration. These positive emotions can make us feel confidence, content, and optimistic about the future. Other times, we experience anger, sadness, and jealousy. These *negative* emotions can lead to feelings of frustration and resentment, and cause unnecessary anxiety.

As noted earlier, negative emotions aren't a problem in and of themselves. They're a natural part of our psyches. Experiencing them does not preclude the development of mental toughness.

The true issue stems from an inability to control these emotions. When we lose control of them, we can too easily become lost in a pool of negativity. The more of our attentional resources we surrender to negative emotions, the less capable we are to remain mentally strong and resolved during times of challenge and hardship.

In short, we're less able to cope with life's difficulties.

Enemy #8: Self-Limiting Beliefs

Each of us possesses a unique set of strengths and weaknesses. Each of us also possesses a set of beliefs regarding our abilities. These beliefs are often out of alignment with reality; we presume personal deficits where none exist. When this happens, our beliefs hamper our ability to take purposeful action toward our goals. In short, they *limit* us.

For example, suppose you're thinking about starting a side business. Following are a few common self-limiting beliefs:

- "I'm too old to start a business."
- "I don't have experience running a business. Without experience, I'll fail."
- "My product idea is stupid. Nobody would buy this product."

These beliefs compose an inaccurate picture. They highlight things that are either untrue or baseless speculation. For instance, you're never too old to start a side business. And millions of people have successfully done so with zero experience. Moreover, there's no way to know if people would buy your product without first offering it to them.

The problem with self-limiting beliefs is that they sabotage us before we get started. They convince us that we're not prepared to achieve what we're trying to accomplish. Unless we overcome these uncharitable thoughts about ourselves, we'll never persist when we encounter hardship and pressure. Consequently, we'll inadvertently inhibit our personal growth and fail to reach our potential.

The Road Forward

We've now covered the background you need to train your brain to endure difficult circumstances and persevere when you're tempted to give up. In *Part II: Pivotal Factors in Developing Mental Toughness*, we'll go through the process together, step by step, toward doing so.

Fair warning: this can be a long, arduous road. It'll require introspection, patience, and consistent application of the tactics and strategies you'll learn in the following pages. But once you reach the end of this road, you'll possess the mental toughness you need to courageously overcome life's adversities in all of its myriad forms.

∼

EXERCISE #1

∼

REVIEW the eight enemies of mental toughness profiled above and consider which ones are wreaking havoc with your cognitive resilience. You may be struggling with one of them in particular. Or perhaps you're struggling with several. Whichever is the case, write them down on an index card. Then, place the index card on your desk where it'll be visible to you.

This short exercise will make you hyper-aware of the challenges you'll need to overcome as you build your mental toughness.

Time required: 5 minutes.

PART II

PIVOTAL FACTORS IN DEVELOPING MENTAL TOUGHNESS

∼

In this section, we'll train to become mentally tough. I'll share practical strategies you can use to master your emotions, improve your resolve, and develop the psychological readiness you need to handle any situation you encounter. The tools you'll receive in this section will also help increase your tenacity and grit when circumstances deviate from your expectations.

This isn't merely about mental stamina. Nor is it just about persistence. It's about developing the cognitive mettle to press forward when things fail to go according to your plans. That requires courage, self-confidence, and mental fortitude.

Facing setbacks and overcoming challenges, and doing so with composure and grace under pressure, is a learned skill. That's terrific news! It means anyone can do it as long as they're committed and willing to put in the time and effort training their mind. To that end, you'll find an exercise at the end of each chapter. Each exercise is designed to help you apply what you've learned. They're simple and easy. And most importantly, they lay a crucial foundation for becoming mentally tough.

Other books heroically detail the theory and psychology behind mental toughness. That's not what we're going to do. On the contrary, we're going to focus on *practical application*. Mental toughness will only be useful to you if you're able to apply it to your daily experience.

Are you ready to master your impulses, control your behaviors, and adjust your mindset so that you respond to adversity in a positive, productive manner? Are you willing to restructure how your brain processes and reacts to difficult situations? If so, let's get to work!

MENTAL TOUGHNESS AND EMOTIONAL MASTERY

~

Our emotions play a vital role in how we face challenges and setbacks. Our ability to function effectively when everything around us is going awry is closely linked to how we process our emotions. If we're unable to control them, our capability to perform under pressure suffers. If we *are* able to exert control, handling mistakes and distress becomes much easier.

This is referred to as our emotional intelligence. It's our ability to understand and manage our emotions in a way that allows us to perform effectively. Rather than stifling our feelings in order to toughen our minds against adversity, we should aim to do the opposite. We should try to recognize how we feel whenever we encounter challenges so we can learn to control our fear, manage our stress, and respond with purpose and determination.

The Value of Self-Awareness

We must know what we feel deep down to become mentally strong. We need to be acutely aware of our thoughts, beliefs, and convictions. We must clarify our values so that our responses to unfavorable circumstances are purposeful.

Becoming mentally strong doesn't require that we detach ourselves from our emotions. On the contrary, we should *embrace* them. That's the only way to truly master them. By acknowledging our fear, frustration, and other negative emotions when things go wrong, we're able to evaluate them, determine their veracity, and regulate the ones that are unrealistic.

Increasing our self-awareness is the first step toward achieving emotional mastery.

The Role of Empathy

Empathy is often misconstrued and oversimplified as "being nice." But it's not merely about being polite or being a good listener. There's a lot more to it. Being empathetic means putting yourself into another person's shoes and acknowledging their emotions in light of their circumstances. You're able to comprehend their thoughts and feelings in that moment.

Although empathy is focused on understanding others, it's an essential skill to building our own mental toughness. We gain unique insight into myriad adverse situations experienced by others. We achieve clarity about such situations that we can use when we encounter them ourselves. And the more empathy we feel toward others, the less likely we are to make uninformed assumptions about their circumstances.

By being empathetic, we can honestly answer the questions:

- "What emotions would I feel in a similar situation?"
- "How would I respond given those emotions?"
- "Is that a reasonable response given my abilities, skills, and knowledge?"
- "What type of person do I want to be when faced with these circumstances?"

Empathy allows us to connect with others. In the process, we're able to learn more about ourselves and candidly examine our own temperament when confronted with complications and distress.

Why Emotional Control Is Critical

Emotional mastery is often misunderstood as meaning to stifle one's emotions. But that belief is incorrect. Emotional mastery entails recognizing our emotions, understanding why we're experiencing them, and *managing* them in a healthy manner.

As mentioned above, we don't want to disassociate ourselves from our feelings. That doesn't lead to mental toughness. Over the long run, disconnecting just makes us more susceptible to anxiety and depression.

Managing our emotions - that is, exerting emotional control - gives us an opportunity to acknowledge them, confront them, scrutinize them, and decide whether what we're feeling is levelheaded given our circumstances.

For example, suppose you've completed an exam at school and received a poor grade. You may feel disgusted with yourself, presuming that you're dense and incapable of doing better. These negative emotions and overly-critical assumptions will wreak havoc with your ability to perform well in the future. Exerting emotional control allows you to explore these emotions and assumptions honestly and determine if they're accurate (spoiler: they're rarely accurate). It gives you a chance to realign your perceptions about your abilities with reality.

Mental toughness is directly connected to how we perceive ourselves and our ability to perform, regardless of our circumstances. Emotions that stem from distress, disappointment, and anxiety hamper us. They slow us down and can even cause us to abandon our intentions when things go wrong. This makes emotion management a requisite skill.

How to Master Your Emotions

Gaining emotional control takes time. Many of us spend our entire lives being heavily influenced by our emotions, even the ones that are unreasonable given our abilities. So, it'll take time to learn to manage them. Following are a few tactics that worked for me. You may find that they work for you, as well.

- Reflect on your feelings, both positive and negative. Acknowledge them.
- Scrutinize negative emotions the moment they surface. Ask yourself, *"Are these emotions reasonable?"* If not, reflect on how these emotions hold you back.
- Meditate for five minutes a day. Observe your emotions without judgement. Mornings are best, but any time is fine.
- Confront your inner critic whenever it "speaks." Investigate its claims to determine if they're accurate.
- Recognize circumstances you *can* influence and circumstances you *can't* influence. Get accustomed to letting go of your frustration regarding the latter.
- Take action, even when you're uncertain of the outcome. This will train your mind to be proactive.
- Try to sleep well, eat well, and exercise. Our physical health influences our emotional health.

Be patient with yourself. No one achieves emotional mastery overnight. The good news is, if you take action every day, you'll eventually be able to manage your emotions whenever you experience difficult situations.

∽

EXERCISE #2

∽

MAKE a list of the negative emotions you typically experience the most when things go wrong. Maybe it's anger. Perhaps it's despair. Or maybe you feel guilty, apathetic, or embarrassed. Whatever the case, write them down.

Now, think carefully about each emotion you've identified on your list. Write a short note next to it that describes how it affects your behavior. For example, feeling angry might cause you to lash out at others. Feeling embarrassed may cause you to retreat mentally, which in turn hampers your ability to take action.

Finally, write a short note next to each negative emotion that describes how you'll respond to it in the future. For example, if you feel angry, you might commit to taking five deep breaths. If you feel embarrassed, you may pledge to examine the reason and determine whether it's rational.

Time required: 15 minutes.

MENTAL TOUGHNESS AND MENTAL RESILIENCE

∼

As we noted earlier, the terms "mental toughness" and "resilience" are often used synonymously. Many people refer to them as if they mean the same thing. In reality, these two attributes are distinct from one another. The distinction is subtle, but it's an important one.

It's essential that we understand the difference between "mental toughness" and "resilience" as we labor to restructure our minds and adjust our instinctive responses to adversity. We'll place both traits under the microscope below. We'll investigate how they differ from one another as well as how that difference affects our training.

We'll then widen our scope. We'll explore how we can use these traits to adapt to our circumstances. We'll also discuss how we can change our perception of failure so we're not discouraged or paralyzed by it.

Mental Toughness vs. Mental Resilience

Again, the difference is subtle. The two are closely related, and so folks who unwittingly conflate them can easily be forgiven for doing so. Having said that, it's important to recognize why using the terms "mental toughness" and "resilience" synonymously is wrong. Using them in such a way obfuscates their difference, and there's value in understanding that difference.

Resilience is the ability to bounce back from unforeseen complications. It's the ability to adapt. For example, suppose you leave your home at a normal time en route to your workplace. Unfortunately, you run into expectedly heavy traffic on the freeway. This setback is sure to make you late for a meeting scheduled that morning.

A resilient person might grit his teeth and curse under his breath, but he'd ultimately adapt to this circumstance. He might seek a different route to his workplace, using his phone's GPS feature. Or he may call his office and reschedule the meeting. Or he might compose an explanation for his tardiness that allows him to avoid others' disapproval.

Mental toughness is a *mindset*. It not only reflects our ability to bounce back from unforeseen complications, but also demonstrates a positive outlook during the experience. It's not just the ability to handle stressful situations. It reflects *how* we handle them.

For example, a mentally tough person caught in unexpectedly heavy traffic might take the opportunity to listen to an inspiring audiobook. In fact, she might be pleased with her circumstance because it *gives* her the opportunity.

While resilient individuals will grudgingly adapt to unanticipated setbacks, mentally tough individuals remain open to *experiencing* such setbacks. They may wish to avoid them, but they realize setbacks are inevitable and ultimately perceive them as challenges to overcome rather than infuriating problems.

It's important to appreciate this difference in mindset. Mental resilience is a useful tool for *coping* with adversity. It gives us the cognitive fortitude to press onward when we confront difficulties. Mental toughness is what allows us to perceive difficulties as *opportunities*. It gives us the confidence and presence of mind we need to use such opportunities to our advantage.

How Catastrophic Thinking Hampers Our Ability to Adapt

It's easy to develop the habit of catastrophic thinking. If we fail to prepare psychologically for the challenges we're sure to face each day, our minds will slowly perceive every obstacle to be more consequential than is true. We'll begin to see setbacks, regardless of their impact and seriousness, as veritable crises.

For example, suppose you're traveling to visit a friend. You catch a flight, confident that you'll arrive at your destination at a predetermined time. During the flight, the captain informs passengers that he must make a detour due to bad weather. The detour will significantly delay your arrival time at your destination.

An individual who lacks mental toughness might panic at this unexpected delay. He may instinctively visualize being unable to contact his friend, who has committed to picking him up at his destination. He might imagine being stuck on the tarmac for hours once his flight finally lands. He may evoke grim images of arriving at his friend's home hours past his expected arrival time, which presages an abysmal night's sleep.

This poor fellow is wallowing in catastrophic thinking.

To become mentally strong, we must guard our minds against this tendency. We must immediately "push back" when our minds entertain worst-case scenarios. Otherwise, we risk being seduced by catastrophic thinking, indulging in unreasonable, imagined outcomes. This frame of mind is wholly incompatible with our ability to recover from setbacks and adapt with purposeful, confident action and a positive outlook.

Change How You Perceive Failure

No one looks forward to failure. After all, failure is evidence of our misconceived expectations or inadequate skills. It's often evidence of both. And that makes failure decidedly unpleasant.

Having said that, we can choose how we regard our failures. Most people are chagrined and shamed by them. They try to hide their failures so others won't discover them. They explain their failures in ways designed to prevent criticism. They might even try to shirk responsibility by pointing their fingers at other people, redirecting blame away from themselves.

These reactions to failure stem from ego. Because failing to accomplish something implies that we're *less* than we expected, we rush to give an account for our lack of success. Oftentimes, these accounts are fallacious, a state of affairs we intuitively rationalize in our haste to camouflage the fact that we've somehow fallen short.

To become mentally tough, we must change how we perceive failure. Rather than dread it, cover it up, and redirect blame, we should embrace it. Failure will never feel pleasant. But we can train ourselves to accept it with the same temperament as we accept success.

Both failure and success are merely outcomes of our decisions and actions. Rather than perceiving the former as "bad" and the latter as "good," we should recognize both as *feedback*. By doing so, we can more easily identify how our decisions and actions are linked to our results. This in turn gives us an opportunity to adjust our expectations and identify deficits in our skills and decision making so we can produce better results in the future.

Perceiving failure as feedback and responding with purposeful action gives us more confidence in our abilities. As we become more confident, we naturally become less apprehensive of unanticipated setbacks. We intuitively know that we can handle any challenge we encounter, even defeat. This awareness allows us to advance beyond mere mental resilience to developing mental toughness and remaining receptive to life's inevitable difficulties.

EXERCISE #3

LIST FIVE RECENT FAILURES. They can be big or small, consequential or insignificant in the grand scheme. Include all relevant details.

Next, describe how you responded in each case. Did you wallow in self-recrimination? Did you berate yourself for an inadequate performance or misguided decision?

Finally, write down how you could have responded in a positive manner in each case. For example, suppose you failed to deliver an important report to your boss on time. A positive response might have been to accept responsibility for missing the deadline, review your workload, and look for ways to better manage your time. Do this for each of the five recent failures.

Once you've completed this exercise, you'll notice how a few fundamental changes in the way you react to failure can increase your confidence and improve your results down the road. This exercise will reveal failures to be merely feedback rather than a final verdict on your capacity to perform.

Time required: 15 minutes.

MENTAL TOUGHNESS IN THE FACE OF ADVERSITY

∼

Hardships are a part of life. You've undoubtedly experienced times when everything has gone wrong to the extent that fate seems to bear a grudge against you. It's unfair. It's unpleasant. And it's almost always out of the blue. During these difficult times your psychological preparedness, emotional resilience, impulse control, and grace under pressure are truly put to the test.

All of us have gone through the gauntlet. All of us can expect to go through it again. That's how life works.

The good news is, adversity strengthens us. Our mental resilience is toughened just as tempering steel with extreme heat toughens its alloys. But in order to take full advantage of this taxing and frustrating process, we must greet adversity with confidence, courage, and composure.

This isn't about willpower. Willpower is a severely limited resource. It gets used up too quickly to rely upon when times get tough. Instead, this is about *character*. Mental toughness requires that we're consistently honest with ourselves, clear about our commitments and convictions, and willing to face difficult situations with a positive mindset.

The Finnish Concept of Sisu

Sisu is a Finnish word. It signifies a particular attitude exemplified by the Finns during times of difficulty. There's no direct English equivalent, but sisu can be roughly described as grim courage in the face of certain failure.

There's a stirring story about the Finns that perfectly describes this admirable frame of mind. At the end of 1939, the Soviet army was about to invade Finland. Negotiations between the Soviet Union and Finland had failed, and war was imminent.

No one expected the Finns to put up much of a fight. The Soviet army outnumbered the Finnish army by a ridiculous factor. It boasted three times the number of soldiers. Moreover, while the Finns had 32 tanks, the Soviet army controlled several thousand. Making matters worse, while the Finns had 114 aircraft, the Soviet army possessed nearly four thousand.

To say the odds were not in the Finns' favor is an understatement. In fact, so lopsided were the odds that Russian leaders, including Nikita Khrushchev, gloated that a single shot fired would compel the Finns to surrender.

But as history shows, that's not at all what happened. The Finns dug in. Armed with outdated weapons and limited resources (ammo, fuel, etc.), they prepared themselves for a vicious and bloody war with no expectation of success. Their steadfastness and bravery epitomized the Finnish concept of sisu. In the face of almost certain failure and death, the Finnish soldiers held their ground. They refused to surrender.

The "Winter War" progressed differently than the Soviet Union predicted. During three months of fighting, the Finns suffered 70,000 casualties while the Soviet army suffered a staggering 400,000. In the end, the Finnish government was forced to accept terms proposed by the Soviet Union. Their weapons were threadbare. Their ammo was exhausted. And 70,000 casualties was an enormous toll on the small country's army.

But the Finns had demonstrated an astonishing degree of mental toughness that shocked everyone. Winston Churchill, in a speech broadcast throughout London in 1940, noted *"Only Finland - superb, nay, sublime - in the jaws of peril - Finland shows what free men can do. The service rendered by Finland to mankind is magnificent."*

How to Embrace Sisu in the Face of Adversity

While few of us will ever need to demonstrate the level of tenacity, grit, and courage exhibited by the Finnish soldiers during the Winter War, we can benefit from their example. We can approach life's inevitable difficulties with a similar attitude. We can accept the challenges we encounter, prepare ourselves to deal with them, and commit to overcoming them. And we can maintain courage and positivity even when the odds are stacked against us.

Following are a few tactics consistent with the Finnish concept of sisu.

First, refuse to let your circumstances overwhelm you. This is easier said than done, of course. Some situations - for example, a diagnosis of cancer - are so dismal and bleak that it's almost impossible to avoid feeling overwhelmed in the beginning. But if you can manage to take back control of your mind when you feel overburdened, you'll be better able to address the obstacles standing in your way.

Second, commit to taking action. It's important to understand your circumstances before responding to them, of course. That requires reflection and contemplation. But eventually, you must act. Even though life is unpredictable and the outcome of your actions and decisions are uncertain, you must adopt an action mindset. This mindset instills courages, enabling you to confront challenges without being paralyzed by your limitations.

Third, practice emotional resilience every day. We're beset with small setbacks on a daily basis. Individually, none are life-changing. For example, we might visit a local Starbucks only to discover they're unable to offer the drink we crave. Or we might unexpectedly get stuck in a traffic jam on our way to the airport. Or we might lose our wallet while shopping. Our reactions, healthy or unhealthy, to these challenges train our minds. If we practice emotional resilience whenever we experience misfortune, we'll reinforce our determination and tenacity.

Fourth, anticipate problems. This not only gives us an opportunity to prepare for them, but allows us to do so with confidence in our ability to overcome them. Imagine being a soldier in the Finnish army in 1939. War is around the corner. The weather is brutal (-40 °C). Your resources are limited. And you're absurdly outnumbered. By anticipating these difficulties, along with their attendant disadvantages, you can take purposeful, confident action to improve your odds.

Let's Sum It Up

Adopting a sisu mindset doesn't mean ignoring your weaknesses. Nor does it entail showing false bravado when confronting insurmountable odds. Rather, a sisu mindset calls for recognizing your circumstances, evaluating your options, and taking determined action toward achieving your desired outcome. It's an acceptance that things are not working in your favor, but a commitment to press forward in spite of that fact.

∼

EXERCISE #4

∼

WRITE down how you normally react to unanticipated problems. Do you wallow in self-pity (e.g. *"why does this always happen to me?"*). Does your inner critic tell you to give up? Do you feel compelled to avoid or ignore the issues at hand? Do you procrastinate taking action due to uncertainty and fear of failure? Do you immediately feel frustrated and angry that life is unfair?

Or do you instinctively roll up your sleeves and prepare psychologically to deal with whatever difficulties you face?

This exercise will reveal your current temperament toward adversity. Keep in mind, there's no shame in how you respond *today* to setbacks and obstacles. After all, the goal of this action guide is to gradually *change* your responses and behaviors when life gets tough. As we've discussed, that's a long road. The purpose of this exercise is merely to get a fix on your mindset in the present.

Time required: 10 minutes.

MENTAL TOUGHNESS AND THE IMPORTANCE OF DELAYING GRATIFICATION

∽

Studies show we're more likely to succeed if we habitually practice self-control. If we delay gratification by way of habit, we stand a much better chance of experiencing success.

"Success" is a murky term because it means something different to each individual. For some, it means earning a large salary. For others, it means being consistently generous, gracious, and humble. Still others measure their success by the health of their interpersonal relationships. For the purpose of this discussion, we'll define success as the achievement of our goals.

Let's clarify what it means to delay gratification. It's the decision to resist enjoying something we crave in the *present* for something we crave even more down the road.

For example, suppose you're trying to lose five pounds. You walk past a pizza parlor and are tempted to purchase a slice. You love pizza and can practically taste it. You now have a decision to make. You can sate your present craving. Or you can resist the temptation and *decide* to steer clear of the pizza in order to meet your goal (losing five pounds).

Notice that it's a decision. You're in control. This means exerting self-restraint is a skill you can learn and hone. As you'll see below, controlling your impulses is paramount to developing mental toughness.

How Developing Impulse Control Increases Mental Toughness

Overcoming setbacks and achieving our goals when we face adversity requires patience. This patience allows us to endure hardships and withstand the emotional and psychological pressure that accompany misfortune. It strengthens our resolve. It increases our grit and tenacity. In encourages us to persist, even when the odds are not in our favor.

When we practice self-restraint, we learn to tolerate discomfort. We train our minds to put up with present unpleasantness for the purpose of achieving our greater goals. In doing so, we inculcate our minds with the idea that we need not satisfy our cravings in the moment. We can resist the impulse to do so.

This improves are cognitive resilience. When we consistently delay gratification, we build our tolerance for discomfort. We grow accustomed to it. This tolerance helps us to persevere rather than surrender to our short-term desires.

For example, suppose you're taking online classes while maintaining a full-time job. After a long, trying day at your workplace, you finally return home. Unfortunately, you have three assignments that are due the following day. If you habitually satisfy your present cravings, you may be unable to resist the temptation to relax on your couch and binge-watch your favorite show on Netflix. However, if you've trained your mind to tolerate discomfort in the present, you'll find it easier to resist the temptation and complete the assignments.

Delaying gratification also improves our ability to ignore distractions. Think of a recent time when you needed to work on something important. For example, you might have needed to complete a report for your job. Or perhaps you needed to complete a long list of household chores. Whatever the case, there were undoubtedly other activities you would rather have been doing. The temptation to indulge in them was a distraction. It threatened to dash your focus. By regularly practicing self-control, you develop the ability to withstand such temptations and remain resolute in your intentions. This is a crucial skill to possess when you encounter unexpected obstacles in the present.

Controlling the impulse to indulge in present pleasure also ingrains within us an important lesson regarding the relationship between effort and reward.

When we repeatedly indulge in immediate gratification, we train our minds to associate low effort with high reward. This conditions our expectations. We become more inclined to surrender to our short-term desires rather than endure discomfort in order to achieve our longer term goals.

For example, we might habitually choose to eat unhealthy fast food because it's easy, convenient, and tasty. Low effort, high reward. Unfortunately, this habit can severely hamper our intention to lose weight, improve cardiovascular health, and build muscle mass.

When we repeatedly *delay* gratification, we form a connection in our minds between self-restraint, effort, and reward. We begin to intuitively recognize that we must exert effort, and in the process control our impulses, to attain what we want. Using our fast food example, we'll feel compelled to resist the siren song of pizza, milkshakes, and fat-laden burgers. Instead, we'll cook healthier meals at home.

It's not easy to control our impulses. Most of us have spent a lifetime catering to them, and suddenly practicing self-restraint can be a frustrating experience fraught with countless slip ups. But delaying gratification is important enough to developing mental toughness that it's worth forming the habit. Following are five tactics that helped me to minimize the struggle.

5 Quick Tips for Delaying Gratification

Fair warning: a few of these tips may not work for you. They proved instrumental for me, but everybody's different. Having said that, I encourage you to try them and gauge whether they're helpful to you. If one or two prove to be useful, I'll consider that a success for both of us.

Tip #1: Clarify your values.

When you recognize what truly matters to you, it becomes easier to prioritize things you'd like to accomplish. That simplifies the decision-making process. It also juxtaposes the importance of your long-term goals with the fleeting pleasure of your short-term desires.

Tip #2: Understand why you'd like to achieve your goal(s).

It's important to have a compelling reason prompting you to take action. Brainstorm that reason for each of your goals.

For example, suppose you wish to lose 10 pounds. Your *reason* may be to feel and look healthier. These motives will encourage you to resist the temptation to eat unhealthy foods in a way that the mere intention to "lose 10 pounds" will not.

Tip #3: Create an action plan.

Using your clarified values and motives, brainstorm a plan that'll guide you through the process of delaying immediate gratification.

For example, suppose you have a tendency to spend every dollar you earn on items for which you have little need (new clothes, new phone, etc.). Create a plan whereby a specific dollar amount from each check is immediately placed into your savings account.

Tip #4: Find a productive alternative to a compulsive desire.

Some temptations are more difficult to resist than others. Simple willpower isn't enough. In such cases, brainstorm another reward to take its place, preferably one with productive value.

For example, you might find pizza irresistible. Junk food is addictive because it triggers the release of dopamine, stimulating the brain's reward center. A productive alternative is physical activity. It too releases dopamine along with endorphins. It may be less fun than eating junk food, but it's a healthier option that feels good, and thereby serves as a fine replacement.

Tip #5: Give yourself a reward for resisting temptation.

Your goal isn't to completely steer clear of pleasurable things. That would be a dismal way to live. Rather, aspire to *develop a habit* of delaying gratification.

The most effective way to develop any good habit is to do so by taking small steps. Each step you successfully take deserves a small reward. The reward trains your brain to repeat the rewarded action.

For example, suppose you're trying to incorporate a daily exercise plan. Rather than forcing yourself to exercise for 30 minutes on Day #1, exercise for three minutes. Then, reward yourself with 10 minutes of leisure reading. Gradually increase the duration of your exercise sessions, and continue rewarding yourself along the way.

I used the above tactics to train myself to delay gratification so that I could pursue my goals without distractions. To that end, they were a significant aid in strengthening my resolve whenever I confronted setbacks and obstacles. Try them for yourself. You may find them to be as effective as I found them to be.

EXERCISE #5

Describe (in writing) a recent incident during which you gave in to a temptation, and in doing so procrastinated or abandoned something you needed to complete. Then describe how your decision made you feel after you had satisfied the craving. Did you feel guilty? Did you experience regret? Did you chastise yourself for surrendering to the temptation?

Next, describe a recent incident during which you *resisted* a temptation and persisted to complete an important task. Then describe how *that* decision made you feel. Did you feel pleased with your resolve? Did you feel empowered?

The purpose of this exercise is to highlight how delaying gratification for the purpose of achieving longer-term goals instinctively feels good to us. It reinforces the idea that controlling our impulses can yield outcomes upon which we place greater value.

Time required: 15 minutes.

MENTAL TOUGHNESS AND YOUR HABITS

~

Our habits sustain us during difficult, challenging times. When life deviates from our plans and we encounter unexpected setbacks, our habits and routines help us to stay on track. They influence our behavior, spurring us forward, practically on autopilot, when we're beset with difficulties and under pressure. When we adopt good habits, our actions and decisions become more consistent. We become less susceptible to our impulses.

The longer our habits have been in place, the more deeply ingrained they are and the more confidence we can have in them. The challenge is in forming them and making them stick.

This section will first discuss how your habits, both good and bad, affect your mental toughness. Then, you'll learn how to develop good habits that last. This system is simple and easy. Most importantly, *it works*. Lastly, we'll explore five daily habits that are pivotal to developing and maintaining mental toughness.

Your Habits Are the Key to Your Mental Toughness

When we think of habits, we typically associate them with action. That is, our habits are things we *do*. But the truth is, they represent much more than that.

Our habits signify what is important to us. They reflect our values and priorities. If we adopt a good diet and regularly exercise, it means our health is important to us. If we meditate each morning, it means we value starting the day with a peaceful, stress-free state of mind. On the other hand, suppose we constantly eat junk food, refuse to exercise, and regularly argue with people online about politics. These habits also suggest our values and priorities.

Perseverance is as much a habit as brushing your teeth before going to bed. It's a behavioral response we train ourselves to carry out in certain circumstances. Like any habit, it has cues that trigger us to take action. The good news is, we can create these cues to help us develop this habit.

This process, developing habits that make our behaviors more consistent, is a vital part in developing mental toughness. It eliminates our need to rely on willpower, motivation, and inspiration, all of which are fickle and fleeting. Instead, we can rely on the routines and systems we design to prompt our behavioral responses to stress and pressure.

With that in mind, let's discuss a simple method for adopting habits that'll strengthen your psychological and emotional resilience.

A Fast-Track Guide to Developing Any Habit (And Making It Stick!)

Leo Babauta, founder of ZenHabits.net, once said with regard to adopting a new habit, "make it so easy you can't say no." There's a lot of wisdom in that simple statement. In fact, it expresses one of the most important principles to developing a new habit: start small.

For example, suppose you'd like to start exercising on a daily basis. You might be enthusiastic and tempted to start your new habit with a 45-minute workout on Day 1. Don't do that. Instead, take baby steps. Start with a 5-minute workout.

This first step is likewise important when developing habits that strengthen your tenacity and resolve. For example, imagine that you feel overwhelmed at your job. You're exhausted and finding it difficult to focus. But you want to develop a habit of perseverance. Rather than rolling up your sleeves and working for hours nonstop, commit to focusing for a 5-minute time chunk. Make it so easy you can't say no.

The next step is to make slow, *incremental* progress. There's no need to grow your new habit by leaps and bounds. This isn't a race. In fact, striving to progress quickly is likely to do more harm than good. For many people, doing so is a recipe for failure.

Take small steps forward. Returning to our previous example, don't try to advance from the initial 5-minute time chunk to working in 45-minute time chunks. Instead, take a small break (perhaps 60 seconds) after the first 5-minute time chunk. Then do another. And another. After you've done that successfully a few times, break up your work into *10*-minute time chunks. Take 2-minute breaks between them. Once you've proven your ability to focus for 10 minutes at a time, work in *15*-minute time chunks separated by *3*-minute breaks.

If you follow this process, you'll eventually build your habit to the point that you should break it down into reasonable portions. For example, let's say you've improved your focus so that you're able to work without distraction for hours on end. That's quite a feat! But it doesn't mean you *should* work for hours on end. In this case, it would be more beneficial to work in relatively short time chunks. For instance, work for 45 minutes, and then take a 10-minute break. Repeat this process four times, and then take a 30-minute break. Working in this manner will help you to maintain your momentum.

Additionally, your focus will suffer less erosion because you're giving your brain a chance to recharge at regular intervals.

The final step in developing a new habit is to design cues that trigger your desired response. It's easy to do. The key is to be consistent.

For example, suppose you're training yourself to continue working after taking short breaks. The problem is, you'd rather abandon your work and watch your favorite show on Netflix. Try this: pick a short, inspiring song. End each break by listening to it. Immediately after the song finishes playing, begin a new work session. This will cause your brain to create an association between the song and your next action (in this case, getting back to work). The next time you hear the song, you'll feel compelled to get back to work.

You control these cues. You get to design them. That means *you* run the show whenever you decide to adopt a new habit.

This simple habit development system doesn't preclude slip-ups. In fact, you almost certainly *will* slip up now and then. Don't worry about it. It's a natural part of the process. Forgive yourself and move forward.

Now that you have a reliable method for adopting new habits, let's explore five that'll increase your mental toughness.

5 Daily Habits That Will Improve Your Mental Strength

Success in any difficult endeavor requires a number of traits, all of which are linked to mental toughness. We've discussed most of them already. They include grit, tenacity, resolve, and a positive state of mind. They also include discipline, persistence, and the willingness to delay gratification.

The following habits align perfectly with these traits. They reinforce them, and in a few cases are instrumental toward building them in the first place. Develop these five habits and you'll find it easier to courageously face any challenges that come your way.

Habit #1: View your past as training for overcoming future adversity.

We tend to let our past define us. We allow earlier events, along with our responses to them, to decide who we are. Our values and convictions are often entwined with what has happened before in our lives.

Sever this connection. Condition your mind to view your past as nothing more than training for the future. Things happened. You responded. Perhaps you made mistakes. Now, it's time to learn from them. Your past is merely instruction that provides you with insight into how best to respond down the road.

Habit #2: Evaluate negative emotions immediately when they arise.

As we discussed previously, negative emotions are not, in and of themselves, unhealthy. On the contrary, research shows they contribute to mental health and psychological well-being. So it pays to acknowledge them.

Having said that, negative emotions can easily hijack your ability to make rational decisions and take purposeful action. They can quickly overwhelm you. So it also pays to assess whether the anger, shame, sadness, panic, and guilt you experience are overblown.

You don't want to suppress negative emotions. But it's important to develop the habit of investigating them the moment they surface.

Habit #3: Build your self-confidence.

Self-confidence is essential to developing mental toughness. After all, it's only possible to press onward during adversity and overcome the fear of uncertainty when you trust in your abilities.

Business magnate Henry Ford once said, "Whether you think you can, or think you can't, you're right." Ford didn't dismiss the role of talent and skill, but instead highlighted the equally important role of confidence. He recognized that our self-assuredness is critical to our success and its absence can easily result in failure.

Habit #4: Practice gratitude.

It's tempting to whine and complain when things go wrong. But it's crucial that we acknowledge two cardinal truths. First, whining and complaining about unfavorable conditions does nothing to resolve them. Second, it can too easily introduce a host of negative emotions that result in further despair and disappointment.

Maintaining a positive mindset is pivotal to facing adversity with courage. Each morning, reflect on things that have gone right for you. Each afternoon, think about everything you have for which to be thankful. Each evening, before you go to bed, contemplate the small victories you enjoyed throughout the day. Practice gratitude daily.

Habit #5: Build a tolerance for change.

Mental toughness requires that you be flexible to your circumstances. When things go wrong, you must be able to adapt in order to act with purpose.

Most of us dread change. We enjoy predictability because it reduces uncertainty. Fear of uncertainty is one of the chief impediments to taking purposeful action.

Building this habit entails leaving your comfort zone. It calls for actively seeking changes that you can incorporate into your life. The upside is that doing so will desensitize you to changing circumstances, increasing your tolerance for them. As your tolerance increases, your fear will naturally erode.

THE GREAT THING about habit development is that you can advance at your own pace. Again, it's best to start with small steps and progress slowly. But each of us is different with regard to what "small" and "slowly" mean. Design a plan that aligns with your existing routines and caters to your available time, attention, and energy.

∼

EXERCISE #6

∼

WRITE down three habits you'd like to develop. Next to each one, write down three things you can do *starting today* to develop the habit.

For example, suppose you want to boost your self-confidence. First, you might commit to saying hello to five stranger each day. Second, you may decide to immediately evaluate negative self-talk whenever your inner critic becomes bold. Third, you might commit to saying no to others, focusing instead on your own projects and responsibilities.

Time required: 15 minutes.

TALENT, ABILITY, AND CONFIDENCE: HOW THEY INFLUENCE MENTAL TOUGHNESS

∼

If the previous section, we briefly mentioned self-confidence as an essential part of developing mental toughness. But the context was limited to habit development. Here, we'll explore self-confidence in greater detail. It has a large enough influence on mental strength, resolve, and psychological resilience under pressure that it warrants a fuller investigation.

We'll start by examining the sources of confidence. Where does it come from? What causes it to grow? What causes it to erode? The answers may surprise you.

Then, we'll discuss why it's important to periodically evaluate our confidence levels. It's sometimes necessary to realign them so they accurately reflect our abilities and knowledge.

Finally, we'll cover five building blocks of self-confidence. This isn't an exhaustive list by any means. But if you incorporate these five elements into your day, your confidence will grow by leaps and bounds. This in turn will help you to respond to uncertain and unfavorable conditions with a strong, levelheaded belief in your ability to overcome them.

Confidence Springs from Ability

Confidence is an expectation that we can prevail over difficult, uncomfortable situations. This self-trust stems, in part, from our abilities, which are comprised of our knowledge base, talents, and areas of proficiency. We're confident when we feel prepared for our circumstances.

For example, suppose you're cooking dinner for a friend. If you've spent years honing your abilities as a chef, you'll feel calm and composed as you prepare the meal. If it's your first time in the kitchen, you might feel a bit of panic.

Confidence also stems from our ability to adapt. Talent and expertise aren't enough. We must be able to pivot when necessary.

Suppose that while preparing a meal for your friend, you discover that you're missing an important ingredient. If you're an experienced chef, you'd adapt to this unexpected predicament by using a suitable substitute. This ability to pivot is a source of confidence. It reinforces your belief in yourself to rectify unforeseen problems and resolve unexpected predicaments.

Realigning Your Confidence Levels with Your Abilities

Sometimes, our confidence levels move out of alignment with our abilities, knowledge, and readiness to adapt to changing conditions. When this happens, it's important that we evaluate ourselves and realign our confidence levels with reality.

If we're overconfident, we might be inclined to take excessive risks, dismiss others' opinions, and ignore our weaknesses. When we confront setbacks and challenges with this frame of mind, we risk being unprepared regardless of our courage.

If we're *under*-confident, we may avoid taking risks, allow others' opinions to control us, and perceive our weaknesses as a harbinger of certain defeat. With *this* frame of mind, we'll be hesitant to respond to setbacks and challenges altogether.

It's difficult to be mentally strong when our confidence levels are unrealistic. Both arrogance and unjustified self-doubt are the enemies of cognitive resilience and resolve. Arrogance might sustain us in the short term, but will lead us off course over the long run. Unjustified self-doubt may prevent us from responding to adversity altogether, fearful of certain defeat.

Given the potential pitfalls of harboring unrealistic confidence levels, it's important to perform a periodic self-assessment. Ask yourself:

- "Are my confidence levels reasonable given my circumstances?"
- "How do I respond to criticism?"
- "Am I immediately inclined to back down when challenged?"
- "Am I eager or reluctant to share my thoughts with others?"
- "When I encounter setbacks, do I instinctively feel fearful and nervous? Or do I feel self-assured? Why?"

This self-appraisal will help you to quickly identify whether your confidence levels need to be realigned. It may also reveal areas in your life that need attention - for example, whether you react to others' criticism in a healthy, sensible manner.

5 Core Building Blocks of Self-Confidence

Improving self-confidence warrants its own book. But there are several elements we can focus on today that'll boost our confidence levels with minimal effort. Most of them involve our mindset. If we embrace them and incorporate them into our day, they'll have a considerable positive impact on our self-trust.

#1 - Willingness to leave your comfort zone.

By leaving our comfort zone, we expose ourselves to unfamiliar situations. Doing so reveals that such situations rarely warrant fear. On the contrary, they offer opportunities to grow, both personally and professionally. They give us a chance to surrender our need to control our circumstances and learn to adapt to new ones.

#2 - Openness to experiencing emotional discomfort.

Self-confidence requires an awareness of our emotions. But it also requires that we build a tolerance to them. The only way to do so is to expose ourselves to the discomfort that accompanies negative emotions.

Many of us tend to suppress emotional pain. But we should remain open to experiencing it as doing so helps us to build resistance to it. This resistance will allow us to remain attuned to negative emotions without being paralyzed by them.

#3 - Habit of self-assessment.

There's considerable value in performing self-evaluations on a regular basis. Earlier, we talked about doing them for the purpose of realigning our confidence levels with reality. Here, we're broadening the scope.

It's important to sit down periodically and reflect on how you've grown. Consider new skills you've learned. Think about peculiar situations in which you found yourself and how you handled them. Take stock of acquaintances you've recently met, recent conversations you've had with strangers, and tasks you performed that were once unfamiliar to you.

We're constantly growing in one way or another. This is especially the case when we leave our comfort zone (see #1 above). The problem is, we often fail to recognize this growth because it happens so gradually.

#4 - Embrace positivity.

Maintaining a positive attitude entails suppressing negative self-talk. It involves highlighting our strengths and celebrating our successes while perceiving our weaknesses and blunders as opportunities to learn and grow.

Sadly, many of us learn to be pessimistic about ourselves thanks to the setbacks and disappointments we experience throughout our lives. This attitude not only hampers our confidence, but also prevents us from growing. The good news is, we can recondition our minds to embrace optimism and positive thinking. In doing so, we can train ourselves to instinctively recognize our ability to overcome adversity.

#5 - Abandon your desire for external validation.

Seeking approval from others hurts your self-confidence. It trains your mind to distrust your motivations and abilities. Instead, your mind learns to refrain from taking action until it receives permission to do so from someone else. Over time, you become wary and begin to harbor misgivings about your ability to perform.

Recognize that you possess unique value. Your knowledge, skills, talents, and adaptability eliminate the need for external validation. As long as your confidence levels are aligned with reality, you can be self-assured and self-assertive when you face uncertainty.

SELF-CONFIDENCE IS one of the keystones to mental toughness. It's difficult to develop the latter without first possessing the former. Fortunately, changing how you see yourself is relatively simple because it's based on recognizing your existing value. Adjusting your self-perception is steeped in actuality rather than the unkind phantoms that result from your inner critic's condemnation.

∼

EXERCISE #7

∼

CREATE a short list of things that regularly hurt your confidence. This might include negative self-talk, a messy workspace, sloppy physical appearance, or an absence of personal boundaries. Everyone is different, and therefore your list will be unique to you.

Next, write down actions you can take to reduce the effect of each item on your self-confidence. Be specific. For example, if you struggle with negative self-talk, you might commit to confronting your inner critic whenever it speaks. If it claims "You're going to fail," you might respond with "You're wrong and here's why."

Finally, address one item a time. Take the actions you listed to lessen the item's impact on your confidence levels. Repetition and consistency are your allies in this exercise.

Time required: 20 minutes.

HOW YOUR ATTITUDE AFFECTS YOUR MENTAL TOUGHNESS

~

Our attitude heavily influences our behaviors. It sets the tone for how we approach difficult situations and respond to them. It largely dictates our psychological resilience when we encounter adversity, and determines the actions we take to overcome - or surrender to - it.

If we have a positive attitude, we're likely to evaluate situations with optimism and confidence. If we have a negative attitude, we're likely to evaluate them with cynicism and fear. Our behavioral responses to setbacks, challenges, and obstacles will spring from these feelings.

This section will do a deep dive into our frame of mind and investigate its impact on our mental toughness. We'll begin by exploring how we perceive ourselves and our circumstances. This piece of the puzzle is more important than might be obvious at first blush.

Overcoming Your Circumstances vs. Expecting Them to Change

When someone tells us to "stay positive," we immediately think of the stereotypical positive thinker who goes through life expecting everything to turn out fine. This individual seems to be oblivious to their circumstances. He ignores life's difficulties, confident they'll simply disappear of their own accord. He experiences no emotional distress because he expects life's misfortunes to sort themselves out.

In short, the stereotypical positive thinker presumes his circumstances will change to suit him. If life were a journey, he sees himself as a mere passenger with little to no influence on the events happening around him.

But this image is mistaken.

Maintaining a positive attitude isn't about harboring baseless optimism. It's not about having faith that things will simply work themselves out. It's about recognizing that we can positively influence our circumstances, prevailing over misfortune and hardship by virtue of our talents, abilities, and capacity to adapt.

This positive outlook, which importantly stems from self-confidence, is a requisite partner to our mental toughness. It dictates how we feel when we encounter complications. It governs how we respond to them. This mindset spurs us to assert ourselves, taking purposeful action rather than remaining passive and hoping for the best.

The Importance of Commitment

When we commit to something, we assign value to it. The outcome we seek becomes, in our estimation, worthy of the time and effort required to pursue it. Our actions and decisions become focused on making it a reality. Our commitment not only encourages us to exert effort toward achieving our desired outcome, but also coaxes us to persist when things fail to go our way.

For example, suppose you start a side business. You commit to making it a success. This commitment encourages you to spend time on it during the evenings and weekends. But it does more than that.

If you've ever run a business, even a small one from a corner of your bedroom, you know a myriad of things can go wrong. And sometimes, they do so suddenly and without warning. Lacking commitment, you might be tempted to throw your hands in the air and say "I give up!" Instead, your pledge to make your business a success prompts you to roll up your sleeves and work to overcome whatever roadblocks you've encountered.

Committing to a task, project, or specific outcome gives us the resilience to stay positive and resolute when we face obstacles. Our commitment helps us to endure when giving up would be easier. It allows us to persist, working toward our goals rather than surrendering them for short-term gratification.

The Willingness to Pursue Continuous Growth

As noted above, a positive attitude gives us confidence that we can overcome adversity. This frame of mind is reinforced whenever we learn new skills (or improve existing ones), absorb new information, or encounter new situations. Our competence and proficiency increases, and with it our self-assuredness.

For this reason, it's vital that we pursue growth in all matters related to our commitments. In fact, pursuing growth in matters that extend *beyond* our commitments is beneficial. Doing so exposes us to unfamiliar situations, which gives us an opportunity to expand our skill set and knowledge base.

People who are mentally tough have a growth mindset. They believe their abilities are not set in stone. Rather, they trust they can learn *new* abilities, often by persevering when life becomes difficult. These individuals are rarely inclined to give up. They perceive their shortcomings as areas that warrant improvement, and setbacks as opportunities to learn from their mistakes.

A growth mindset is integral to cognitive resilience. It's an essential component of a positive attitude. The underlying belief that we can constantly improve ourselves and thereby achieve things that were impossible for us in the past is essential to becoming mentally strong. It reinforces our self-confidence, which amplifies our willingness to stay the course when we encounter adversity.

There's one last element that directly impacts our attitude, and with it our capacity for resilience: gratitude.

The Art of Being Grateful

Many people wallow in self-pity. They grumble about how life is unfair and why their circumstances prevent them from accomplishing their goals. These folks are preoccupied with their own unhappiness. They indulge in victimhood rather than acknowledging their talents and abilities. This frame of mind leads to perpetual frustration and can even open the door to depression.

Unsurprisingly, people who habitually feel sorry for themselves often give up when they're confronted by challenges.

It's important to recognize that self-pity is a choice. It's an attitude we adopt rather than one that overtakes us. Once we adopt this negative attitude, it can quickly gain a foothold in our minds, prompting us to instinctively blame our failures on our circumstances.

This frame of mind is contrary to developing mental toughness.

When we express gratitude, we underscore the fact that we possess resources, both internal and external, that'll help us to endure failure, misfortune, and hardships. We give voice to our appreciation for our talents and abilities. In doing so, we elevate our self-confidence while remaining open to experiencing further growth.

The next time you begin to feel a twinge of self-pity, do the following:

- Question the reality of your emotional state. Is the self-pity reasonable or are you overlooking your potential?
- Resist the urge to complain to others. Complaining merely reinforces the unhealthy tendency to seek validation.
- Reflect on the good things in your life.
- Tell a friend or family member that you love and appreciate them. You'll make that person's day and you'll feel good, too. It's a win-win!

These simple activities will quickly dispel self-pity. That'll relieve the psychological and emotional pressure caused by your circumstances, and allow you to take purposeful action to prevail over them.

EXERCISE #8

WRITE down five things you did today that relied upon your current skill set and knowledge. Examples might include creating a report at your job, taking an exam at school, or fixing a broken appliance at home. This will reinforce the reality that you possess productive resources (know-how, expertise, adaptability, etc.)

Time required: 5 minutes.

EXERCISE #9

WRITE down five things you learned today. Examples might include learning a new word or phrase, how to cook a new dish, or how to play a new song on your guitar. This exercise emphasizes the fact that you're always growing and improving in some way.

Time required: 5 minutes.

EXERCISE #10

WRITE down five things for which you're thankful today. This might include your job, your relationship with your spouse, or the ability to keep your refrigerator stocked with food. This exercise trains your mind to express gratitude, the bane of self-pity.

Time required: 5 minutes.

MENTAL TOUGHNESS AND YOUR INNER CRITIC

∼

Your inner critic is a shrewd adversary. It knows that it doesn't have to yell to get your attention. It doesn't have to scream to pummel your psyche, wear down your self-confidence, and encourage you to adopt a negative attitude. Your inner critic *whispers* its dubious, condemning claims. And that's enough. These whispers can produce such great fear and anxiety that we become paralyzed and unable to take action.

Each of us has our own inner critic. It sits comfortably in the background, waiting for an opportunity to criticize our actions, judge our work, and denounce our decisions. We must learn to silence this internal voice. Otherwise, we risk being overwhelmed by its persistent assault. The negative self-talk it produces throughout each day can take a severe emotional and psychological toll.

Below, we'll discuss how to recognize negative self-talk. (It's not always obvious.) Once you know the signs, you can take steps to stop your inner critic from bullying you. We'll cover several tips you can use *today* toward that end.

Common Signs Your Inner Critic Is Restless

Your inner critic is like a small child. It gets bored easily. When it gets bored, it can become disruptive. Unfortunately, its antics are often difficult to spot. Your inner critic does its most effective work while staying hidden in the background.

Having said that, there are a few telltale signs that betray its tricks.

First, your inner critic excels in catastrophic thinking. It'll make questionable claims, whispering that "you're going to fail," "you're going to lose your job," and "they're going to hate you." These claims seem reasonable at first. We're inclined to believe them, assuming the voice in our head is trying to protect us.

Second, your inner critic is adept at making you feel guilty. It'll justify its claims that you're incompetent by pointing out things you've done or decisions you've made that led to failure in the past.

Third, your inner critic uses extreme generalizations and ridiculous absolutes. Following are a few examples:

- "You'll NEVER succeed."
- "EVERYONE will think you're an idiot."
- "You fail at EVERYTHING."
- "You ALWAYS say the wrong things."
- "NOBODY cares what you think."

Fourth, it draws a hard line in the sand between success and failure. You either succeed or you fail. There's no in-between. Worse, your inner critic sets the criteria for success unreasonably high. For example, if you receive a "B" on an exam, you've failed. If you prepare a meal that's slightly less than perfect, you've failed. If you give a presentation at work and don't receive enthusiastic accolades from *every* attendee, you've failed.

Fifth, your inner critic predicts the future with an air of finality. And the future it predicts is usually negative. For example, the girl you intend to ask out on a date will say no, never, or not even if you were the last man on earth. The marketing plan you intend to show a client will be summarily rejected. The side business you'd like to start will fail miserably, and you'll become a laughing stock amongst your friends in the process.

Your inner critic is almost certainly your most unpleasant, obnoxious, and disrespectful acquaintance. It's time to quash the negative self-talk.

5 Things You Can Do Today to Silence Your Inner Critic

Following are simple things you can do that'll help stifle the negative internal dialogue that's wreaking havoc with your confidence, self-worth, and mental toughness. All of them are easy and take minimal time and effort. I encourage you to try them today.

#1 - Scrutinize negative thoughts the moment they surface.

In 2005, the National Science Foundation published an article claiming we have between 12,000 and 50,000 thoughts a day. It went on to claim that 80% of these thoughts are negative. Whether or not these claims are true (and some have expressed skepticism), we *do* experience a lot of negative thoughts throughout the day. So many, in fact, that we develop a blind spot to them, allowing them to simmer under the surface.

Whenever your inner critic "speaks," examine its claim. Don't simply ignore it. And certainly don't accept what it says at face value. Recognize its claims as destructive to your emotional mastery, psychological readiness, and mental toughness.

#2 - Ask for evidence.

If your inner critic condemns you as a failure, predicts catastrophe, or tries to convince you that you're ill-equipped for a planned task or project, ask for evidence. It'll probably trot out things you did unsuccessfully in the past. But remember, we're always growing and improving. Failure in the past doesn't limit our success in the future. Given this, such evidence is shaky at best and outright fallacious at worst.

#3 - Come up with a rational response to every overgeneralization your inner critic makes.

Recall from above the ridiculous absolutes your inner critic trades in: ALWAYS, NEVER, NOBODY, EVERYONE, etc. Claims based on these absolutes are almost always gross exaggerations with little merit. One of the best ways to dismiss them is to counter them with a reasonable response.

For example, suppose you want to improve at public speaking. If your inner critic is feeling emboldened, it might claim "you'll NEVER be able to speak in public." The claim is ludicrous. You can counter it with "if I practice enough, I will definitely improve." This is an irrefutable expectation. And it immediately discharges your inner critic's baseless claim to the contrary.

#4 - Stop spending time with negative people.

Each of us knows at least one person who is chronically negative. They're pessimistic, cynical, and habitually demoralized. They complain, criticize, and can put a negative spin on *anything*. Being around these folks is emotionally exhausting. Worse, their negativity can be highly contagious. Spend enough time with them and you'll find your own positive mindset leaking away.

    Guard your time. Don't allow negative people to monopolize it. Instead, spend more time with those who have a persistently positive outlook. These folks tend to be confident, upbeat, optimistic, and productive. Being around them will reinforce your emotional and cognitive strength.

#5 - Advise an imaginary friend.

We tend to be kinder to those we care about than to ourselves. For example, we might say to ourselves after making a simple mistake "Well, *that* was stupid, dummy." But we wouldn't say that to a friend or loved one. We'd be more supportive and encouraging. For instance, we might tell him or her "It's just a small mistake. We all make them. Don't let it get you down." We might even try to make them feel better by describing a similar - or even *bigger* - blunder we recently made.

The next time your inner critic makes a rude, unjustified claim, imagine that you're giving advice to a friend. But give it to yourself instead. Be kind and sympathetic. You'll find that being so will make it easier to forgive yourself and move on with resolve.

IN MICRO DOSES, you inner critic can serve a useful purpose. It can highlight things you've done wrong so you have an opportunity to adjust and improve. The problem is, your inner critic never restrains itself. It inevitably finds fault in everything, slowly whittling away your emotional strength and mental toughness. However, here's the good news: Once you recognize your inner critic's machinations (and they're easy to recognize once you know its tricks), you can silence it.

∼

EXERCISE #11

∼

WRITE down 10 examples of negative self-talk you've experience during the past week. They can be small or big, mildly annoying or utterly abusive.

For example, has your inner critic told you any of the following?

- "You'll never lose weight."

- "Nobody likes you."
- "You look awful in that outfit."
- "Your friend Mark ignored your text. He's angry with you."
- "You're not as capable as those people."
- "Your boss is going to fire you."
- "Your coworkers don't respect you."
- "You're an idiot."

Once you've written down 10 examples from the past week, write down a reasonable response to each one. For example, next to "you'll never lose weight," you might write "if I eat less junk food and take a 30-minute walk each day, I'll slowly lose weight."

This exercise reveals your inner critic's claims to be bogus. Moreover, it trains your mind to instinctively perceive its claims with suspicion.

Time required: 20 minutes.

THE ROLE OF WILLPOWER AND MOTIVATION

Let's start with a couple definitions. Willpower is the ability to delay gratification with the intent of working toward your goals. For example, suppose your goal is to lose 15 lbs. Resisting the urge to eat a donut would be an expression of willpower. It's a demonstration of self-control.

Motivation is trickier to define. At its simplest, it's an impulse to effect change. Such change might come in the form of achieving a goal (e.g. changing ourselves by losing 15 lbs.). It can also include improving our circumstances (e.g. completing our to-do lists to relieve stress), raising awareness about a particular issue (e.g. the treatment of animals), or advancing a cause that's important to us (e.g. climate change). It's an amalgamation of engagement, behavior, and according to psychologists, instinct.

As I said, it's a little trickier to define than willpower. For the purpose of this book, we'll limit the context of motivation to involve that which spurs us to improve our circumstances.

With that said, how important are willpower and motivation to developing mental toughness? What are their respective roles? We can only answer these questions once we understand how willpower and motivation work.

The Practical Mechanics of Willpower

Have you ever noticed that it's easier to make difficult decisions in the morning than in the evening? For example, let's say you get out of bed in the morning and you're faced with the choice of going for a jog or watching TV. It's relatively easy to make the hard choice and slip on your running shoes. Now, suppose you've arrived home after a long, stressful day at work. You're presented with the same choice: jog or watch TV. It's more difficult to delay gratification. If you're like me in that situation, you'll choose to watch TV.

That's how willpower works. It's like fuel in our tank. It gets used up as the day progresses. By the end of the day, the tank runs dry and our resolve to make hard choices melts.

Years ago, the peer-reviewed *Proceedings of the National Academy of Sciences* (PNAS) published a study that investigated the influence of external factors on eight judges' parole decisions.[1] The authors looked at more than 1,000 such decisions and discovered an interesting trend. The further the day had progressed when a decision was made, the greater the likelihood that a request for parole was denied. The judges evidently found it more difficult to make tough decisions, erring on the side of request denial, as the day moved forward.

The authors found another interesting tidbit of data. The judges were more likely to grant parole during the brief period that immediately followed their lunch break.

One explanation for this phenomenon is decision fatigue, a form of mental fatigue. The more decisions we make, the less willpower (i.e. fuel in our tank) we have to make subsequent decisions. The absence of willpower makes it difficult for us to make hard choices, and we instead choose the easier option.

Keep these mechanics in mind as we turn our attention to motivation.

The Power (And Fleeting Nature) of Motivation

Have you ever been motivated to the point that you felt absolutely *compelled* to do something? Maybe the feeling surfaced after you listened to a rousing speech. Or perhaps you were presented with a unique opportunity to achieve your dream. Or maybe your motivation to act was prompted by an ultimatum (for example, your boss may have told you'll lose your job if you fail to meet your daily sales quota).

Motivation can be a powerful impetus for taking purposeful action. Changing our circumstances usually comes at a price. This price might be imposed on our comfort, our time, or our resources. When we're highly motivated to bring about a particular change, we're willing to pay a higher price to do so (e.g. work harder, invest more time, or sacrifice more resources). Conversely, when we're not motivated, the price we're willing to pay plummets.

And this is the problem with motivation. It's difficult to harness. And if we're unable to harness it, we can't take advantage of it on a consistent basis. It's an unreliable resource.

Having said that, there's a "trick" you can use to train your mind to act even if you lack both willpower and motivation. It's a reliable way to prompt yourself to take action even when you prefer to choose a more immediately-gratifying option.

And the best part? This "trick" dovetails perfectly with our development of mental toughness.

How to Take Action without Willpower and Motivation

Let's not dance around it.

The key to taking action in the absence of willpower and motivation is to rely on habits. Create routines and rituals that spur you to take action on autopilot. Once these routines are in place, you'll no longer be a powerless victim to decision fatigue. You'll no longer need to wait to feel motivated to pursue a change in your circumstances. Your habits will prompt you. And the more consistent your habits, the easier it'll be for you to make choices that align with your goals.

Let's return to our example of returning home after a tiring, stressful day at work. You can either go for a jog or watch TV. If you want to stay physically fit and you normally go for a jog after work, you'll find it easier to do so on a consistent basis. The habit is in place. Your mind is accustomed to the existing routine, and will prompt you to act in accordance with it even if sitting on your couch and watching TV is more immediately gratifying.

We discussed the importance of habits earlier (in the section *Mental Toughness and Your Habits*). We talked about how they sustain us during times of adversity. This is the reason they're a crucial component in our development of mental toughness.

Here, it was important to juxtapose their reliability in contrast to that of willpower and motivation. In short, you can *always* rely on habits.

Motivation is a topic that warrants a deep dive. There's a lot of science behind it, and it's incredibly interesting. But that discussion lies far beyond the scope of this book.

∿

EXERCISE #12

∿

WHENEVER YOU FEEL the impulse to do something you enjoy, meditate for five minutes before acting on the impulse. Set a timer. Then close your eyes and focus on your breathing.

This simple exercise trains your mind to exert self-control. It's an easy way to grow accustomed to discomfort and delay gratification without experiencing significant inconvenience.

Time required: 5 minutes.

EXERCISE #13

WRITE down five things that motivate you to take action. Perhaps it's reading a self-improvement book. Maybe it's listening to a certain type of music. Or you might feel especially motivated when you spend time with like-minded people.

Next, write down five things that cause your motivation to evaporate. This might include eating sugary foods, catering to your perfectionist tendencies, or spending time with pessimistic people.

This exercise will reveal environmental influences on your motivation. Once you're aware of them, you can make sensible adjustments that better serve your longer term goals.

Time required: 10 minutes.

---

1 Avnaim-Pesso, Liora, Danziger, Thai, & Levav, Jonathan (2010). Extraneous factors in judicial decisions. Proceedings of the National Academy of Sciences. 6889-6892.

https://www.pnas.org/content/pnas/108/17/6889.full.pdf

THE ROLE OF SELF-DISCIPLINE

Back when I worked in Corporate America, I started a side business. I ran it from my living room. I'd wake up at 4:00 a.m. each morning and work on the business until it I needed to head into the office. Then, upon returning home in the evening, I'd work on it again. I'd finally go to bed at midnight, sleep for four hours, and start the cycle over the following morning.

I did this for years (coffee was my closest friend).

The thing that made this possible (besides coffee) was self-discipline. It wasn't willpower. It wasn't motivation. It was the act of forcing myself to do that which did not come naturally to me, day after day after day. It was a matter of controlling my impulses, forgoing immediate gratification, and tolerating extreme inconvenience.

It wasn't healthy. Not by a long shot. While I was able to grow my business, my health, both emotional and physical, suffered as a result.

But I learned an important lesson about discipline by running this self-imposed gauntlet. First, I discovered that we can force ourselves to endure just about anything if we're sufficiently focused on our goal. This perseverance can help us prevail over procrastination, indecision, fear, and laziness.

Second, I learned that self-discipline was a prerequisite to mental toughness. You can't develop the latter without first developing the former. In a way, building self-discipline is training for becoming mentally tough. It's a form of boot camp.

I'll share in this section what worked for me in building discipline. If you're already hyper-disciplined, feel free to skip to the next section. But if you have trouble sticking to your commitments, working toward your goals, and tolerating inconvenience, you'll find this section helpful.

Let's start by examining the difference between self-discipline and willpower.

Self-Discipline vs. Willpower

Many people think self-discipline and willpower are the same thing. But you already know them to mean different things. As we noted in the previous section, willpower is a finite resource that quickly wanes. Like the fuel in our vehicles, the more we use it, the more quickly it dwindles away.

In my Corporate America days, back when I was building my side business, friends and family members used to remark "you have a lot of willpower." But that wasn't truly the case. Willpower could never have sustained me through my years of self-inflicted punishment (sleep deprivation and delayed gratification).

Certainly, willpower is useful. The temporary burst of energy spurs us to take purposeful action that's contrary to our immediate desires. But doing so over and over in a structured manner? That requires self-discipline.

Willpower will help you to get out of bed at 5:00 a.m. tomorrow morning when you'd rather stay under the warm covers. *Self-discipline* will help you to do so *every* morning.

Willpower will give you the self-control you need to resist eating junk food this afternoon. *Self-discipline* will give you the self-control you need to abstain from junk food for the foreseeable future.

Willpower is like that friend who's occasionally there for you but mostly not. He (or she) cannot be relied upon. Self-discipline is like that friend who's *always* there for you, regardless of the circumstances. Once you develop that "friendship," you can rely on it with complete and utter confidence.

So, let's talk about how to develop it.

5 "Secrets" to Mastering Self-Discipline

There are no secrets to developing discipline. It requires time and effort, just like building any habit. And like building any other habit, you can expect failure and frustration to be a part of the process.

Knowing this ahead of time is helpful. If you stumble - assuming you're not a robot, you *will* stumble on occasion - it'll lessen the disappointment. And that'll make it easier to forgive yourself and get back in the saddle.

The following five "secrets" (I say this with my tongue firmly planted in my cheek) proved invaluable for me while I was striving to build self-discipline. I'm willing to bet they'll prove useful to you, as well.

"Secret" #1: Create a temptation-free environment.

You'll find it easier to resist temptations when you remove them from your environment. For example, suppose you have difficulty resisting junk food. The solution is to get rid of all the junk currently in your home, office, cubicle, and desk. Access stimulates our impulses. Lack of access helps us to control them.

"Secret" #2: Take small steps forward.

Again, this is just like building any other habit. Don't aspire to become hyper-disciplined overnight. Instead, plan to take small, purposeful, consistent actions over the course of weeks (and perhaps months). And then, celebrate the modest victories along the way.

Taking small steps and acknowledging small successes makes forward progress easier and more rewarding. It also trains your mind to recognize that you're in the driver's seat. You're in control.

"Secret" #3: Create an action plan.

Don't leave this to happenstance. Come up with a feasible strategy that prompts you to take focused action on a consistent basis.

For example, let's say you want to start journaling each morning. Don't assume you'll do so just because it's your intention. Plan ahead by putting "journaling" on your calendar. Block off a 15-minute time chunk each morning (e.g. from 6:30 a.m to 6:45 a.m.) and consider it to be a can't-miss appointment with yourself.

"Secret" #4: Grow accustomed to short-term unpleasantness.

Short-term discomfort is an unavoidable part of developing self-discipline. It's important to learn to tolerate malaise, delaying gratification in service to our goals. The alternative is to immediately cater to our impulses. For instance, if we crave junk food, we'd simply eat it. If we get sick of our job, we'd quit. If we get annoyed at a friend, we'd stop being friends with that individual. That's the *opposite* of discipline.

When you feel frustrated, annoyed, or otherwise troubled, embrace these feelings. Don't avoid them. Acknowledge them without giving in to them. The more you do so, the more you'll strengthen your impulse control.

"Secret" #5: Commit to doing nothing but the task in front of you.

Novelist Raymond Chandler once explained his writing discipline to his friend Alex Harris. Chandler wrote in a letter, *"Either write or nothing.... I find it works. Two very simple rules, a: you don't have to write. b: you can't do anything else."*

This perspective was a remarkable help for me when I was working in Corporate America and building a business on the side. Bleary-eyed and waiting for the coffee to kick in, I would tell myself, *"You don't have to build this website right now. You choose not to do so. But you have to sit here and do nothing else."* I invariably got to work.

SELF-DISCIPLINE COMES IN MANY FORMS. But it ultimately boils down to resisting our impulses and carrying out our plans regardless of the attendant inconvenience. We can learn to do this, and in so doing pave the way to bolster our mental toughness.

∾

EXERCISE #14

∾

WRITE down 15 things that require discipline to resist or discipline to carry out. These should be things you encounter on a regular basis. Following are a few examples to get you started:

- washing dishes that are sitting in the sink
- forgoing watching TV after a long day
- making the bed after you get up in the morning
- going for an early morning run
- abstaining from gossip at the office
- meditating in the morning

- ignoring your phone while working

Over the next week, commit to practicing self-discipline by doing the things you'd rather avoid, and avoiding the things (at least, temporarily) you'd prefer to do. This exercise will train you to endure short bouts of discomfort.

Time required: 10 minutes.

HOW TO REJECT THE DESIRE TO GIVE UP

~

Let's do a quick review. We've talked about willpower and motivation. You learned how they work and why they're unreliable. We also talked about self-discipline. You learned that it's an important stepping stone to mastering mental toughness (along with a few tactics that'll help you to develop it).

In this section, we'll take these concepts to their logical conclusion.

The core aspect of mental toughness is the ability to deal with life's setbacks and challenges when we encounter them. It's about refusing to give up. It's about sticking to our plans and managing our emotions when things go awry.

Mental toughness and our refusal to surrender to defeat and despair is crucial when we experience extreme adversity and hardships. For example, it's helpful when we lose our jobs, go through divorce, or see loved ones pass away. But it's just as helpful when we're forced to weather life's smaller predicaments. In fact, it's these less momentous situations that give us an opportunity to apply - and benefit from - mental toughness on a daily basis.

For example, suppose you're trying to stick to a healthy diet. One day, something triggers your cravings for junk food and you spend the entire afternoon binge-eating donuts, ice cream, and chocolate. You'll no doubt feel disappointed in yourself. Your inner critic will tell you to abandon your diet, trying to convince you that you lack the resolve to stick to it. If you're mentally tough, you'll refuse to quit. You'll consider the day a temporary setback, and resume your diet the following day.

We experience these smaller predicaments every day. We encounter them at our jobs, in our homes, while we're running errands, and when we're spending time with friends and loved ones. This is where mental toughness pays massive dividends. In our daily lives, when we inevitably encounter life's small, yet distressing, difficulties.

Let's now take a closer look at why we give up.

5 Most Common Reasons We Give Up

We don't like to think of ourselves as quitters. But most of us have, at some point in our lives, abandoned goals due to the obstacles we faced at the time. We gave up. We weren't willing to persevere.

The important question is why? Once we uncover the reasons, we can deal with them in a productive manner. We can adjust our mindset, develop healthier habits and routines, and thereby short-circuit the processes that prompt us to surrender when life becomes difficult.

Following are five reasons most people give up when they encounter setbacks.

#1 - We don't "own" our commitments.

Have you ever set a goal that was unimportant to you? You probably didn't take it seriously.

I've done this more times than I can remember. And inevitably, I abandoned those goals at the first sign of difficulty. That's what happens when we don't feel a true sense of ownership for the things we set out to accomplish.

This isn't to suggest you fully commit to every goal you set. On the contrary, goals *should* be abandoned when they no longer align with your longer term aspirations. But if you want to persevere when life gets tough, you must own the outcome you desire. You must feel accountable for it.

#2 - We train ourselves to surrender to temptation.

In the same way we develop *good* habits, we also develop *bad* habits. One of these bad habits is to give in to our impulses. The more we do it, the stronger the habit becomes and the quicker we're willing to give up when faced with adversity.

For example, if you've ever tried to maintain a healthy diet (and who among us hasn't?), you've experienced the temptation of junk food. Perhaps you even rationalized giving in to it (e.g. "Just one little bite won't hurt me."). The problem is, the mind has a sneaky way of convincing us to make such small concessions over and over. As we do so, we train ourselves to respond to our impulses.

Conversely, if we manage to resist our impulses over and over, we train our minds to tolerate short-term discomfort. And that reduces our tendency to give up at the first hint of temptation.

#3 - We're easily distracted.

Our minds always search for the easier path. That's rational. Why should we put in more effort than necessary to achieve our desired outcome? Why should we endure more stress than necessary toward that end? In short, why should we put ourselves through distress and discomfort if there's no need to do so?

Again, this mindset is entirely rational. So when we encounter obstacles, our minds immediately look for paths that offer less resistance. The problem is, there are countless distractions that offer such paths. Examples include social media, Netflix, our phones, and our various hobbies. We can even be distracted by easier goals.

When we're distracted, we're more likely to abandon tasks and projects when we encounter difficulties. We look for easier activities that pose less trouble and fewer complications.

Fortunately, we can train ourselves to ignore distractions. It takes time, just like developing any good habit.

#4 - We're unclear about the reward.

Everything we do, we do with purpose. We work toward achieving a particular outcome because that outcome carries a reward that is important to us.

For example, we study hard to get good grades in college because graduating with honors improves our job prospects. We resist the urge to eat junk food because eating healthy allows us to lose weight and feel more energetic. We invest our time, effort, and emotions into select relationships because we want these relationships to be rewarding over our lifetimes.

When we're clear about the rewards we'll enjoy for our efforts, we're more inclined to endure the hardships we face along the way. When these rewards are *unclear* to us, we're more inclined to give up. We rightfully ask ourselves "What's the point of enduring this misery?"

This is the reason we should be clear about the payoff we stand to enjoy for anything we do. Awareness of this payoff will help us to resist the urge to give up when complications surface.

#5 - **We entertain excessively optimistic expectations.**

It's good to be optimistic. In fact, as we discussed in the section *Top 7 Traits of Mentally Tough People*, optimism is critical to developing mental toughness. But it must be practical and cautious.

When we're overoptimistic, we fail to anticipate potential obstacles and challenges. We develop a blind spot for them. Consequently, we're unprepared to respond to such impediments in a productive, purposeful manner. This inevitably leads to discouragement and frustration, which makes us more likely to give up.

Of course, there's no way to reliably predict everything that might go wrong during the course of a particular endeavor. But we can guard our minds against overoptimism by starting with the expectation that things can - and often *do* - go wrong. That alone will help us to resist the impulse to give up if (or when) things do so.

Ask Yourself These 5 Questions When You Feel like Quitting

Whenever you're tempted to give up, it's helpful to ask yourself a series of probing questions. These questions, which you'll find below, will clarify whether the urge to give up stems from an emotional impulse or a reasoned decision.

As noted above, giving up *can* be a sensible option, particularly when a goal is no longer important to us. But if an outcome *is* important to us, we should investigate whether the desire to give up makes sense. And that entails asking several pointed questions to get to the heart of the matter.

#1 - Why do you want to quit?

Does the endeavor require too much effort? Too much time? Does it involve too much stress? If you know why you want to quit, you can make a reasoned decision regarding whether doing so is pragmatic.

#2 - Does the reward adequately compensate you for the discomfort?

If you're putting yourself through the proverbial wringer, the reward must be worthwhile. If it's not, why endure the anguish and grief? If the reward *is* worthwhile, asking yourself this question provides a helpful reminder.

#3 - What is your purpose?

It's easy to forget why something is important to us. We get lost in the *process* of achieving our desired outcome and start to neglect the reason we wanted to achieve it in the first place.

Asking yourself this question gives you an opportunity to revisit your purpose. If it's still important, you can resolve to press on. Otherwise, you can reasonably and confidently without regret decide to abandon the endeavor.

#4 - Are you tempted to give up due to weak resolve or because your outlook has changed?

When I first learned how to build a website, I was excited to learn everything I could about the underlying code. But along the way, my outlook changed. My interest in *building* a website waned while my interest in *having* a website that people enjoyed visiting became a much higher priority.

So I abandoned that original endeavor and hired someone to build my website. I gave up on my goal of learning the code. But my reason for doing so was sound.

If you're tempted to give up, ask yourself this crucial question. If your vision has changed, giving up may be the right option. However, if the impulse stems from weak resolve, revealing it as so can spur you to renew your commitment.

#5 - Will you regret the decision to give up?

Asking this question entails predicting how Future You will feel as a result of the decisions you make today.

For example, suppose you're trying to stick to a healthy diet. If you decide to abandon this endeavor, how will you feel about the decision one year from today? Will Future You have zero regrets? Or will Future You kick yourself for making that decision?

If the latter is likely to be the case, this is the time to renew your commitment rather than surrender to the impulse to give up.

AGAIN, there's nothing wrong with abandoning a task, project, or goal if it no longer dovetails with your longer term outlook. But if you're tempted to give up due to lack of resolve, it's important to investigate the impulse and ask yourself probing questions to determine if you should reject it.

∼

EXERCISE #15

∼

THINK of someone who overcame tough odds and significant adversity by virtue of their will, resolve, and tenacity. This individual can be a friend, family member, acquaintance, or even a celebrity you've never met.

For example, I have a friend who built a thriving company despite personal health issues. Additionally, a close family member struggled for years with severe financial issues, and overcame them to build a successful, rewarding life for him and his family.

An example of a celebrity is basketball great Michael Jordan, who was unceremoniously cut from his high school basketball team. He persevered to become one of the sport's most celebrated players.

Reflect on the individual's efforts, frustrations, and ultimate success.

Don't compare yourself to this person. Simply contemplate the resilience and grit he or she displayed in climbing their personal mountain.

Now, describe a personal situation in which you gave up and now regret your decision. Write down three things you could have done to persevere with the same attitude as the individual you just contemplated.

Time required: 15 minutes.

THE UPSIDE OF BOREDOM

~

Most of us grew up thinking that boredom was something to avoid. We were told it stemmed from an absence of curiosity, lack of interests, and inability to entertain ourselves. We were told "only boring people get bored."

Naturally, boredom took on negative connotations. It's unsurprising that, in adulthood, boredom leaves us feeling unsettled. Some of us may even experience a niggling sense of guilt from being in such a state. If we're bored, we're not busy or productive enough, right?

Wrong.

The truth is, there's nothing bad about boredom. In fact, it can be a gift. Rather than trying to fill the void, we should enjoy - even celebrate - the downtime. It's an opportunity to think about our circumstances, contemplate the day, and improve our self-awareness. These activities bolster our psychological readiness, and in doing so increase our mental toughness.

In this section, you'll learn that boredom is not only inevitable, but also a necessity. It's a fundamental part of developing expertise in any skill, a process that raises our self-confidence. You'll also receive several tips that'll help you to get comfortable with boredom and even learn to embrace it.

Boredom Is a Corequisite of Mastery

Think of a skill you've mastered. Consider the time and attention you devoted to it. Reflect on the experience of practicing your craft. There were undoubtedly times when you felt bored during the process.

The brain is stimulated by *new* things. We're excited by the prospect of learning new skills and putting them to use. The trouble is, mastering a skill requires practice and repetition. And when you practice something over and over, it starts to become boring. You must continue to put in the time to maintain your proficiency. But the brain essentially goes to sleep, working on autopilot.

In this way, boredom is a precondition of mastery. No one masters anything without experiencing boredom in the process.

For example, suppose you've mastered playing the guitar. You've devoted thousands of hours to memorizing every chord and scale, playing them cleanly, and learning music theory to deepen your understanding about how everything fits together. After years of training, you're an expert. You've surely experienced times of intense boredom along the way.

That's how mastery works. If you plan to develop expertise in a skill or craft, boredom should be an expectation.

Mastery Is a Necessity for Mental Toughness

Why is mastery important to us in the context of developing mental toughness? Because mastery gives us a sense of control. The more control we feel we possess, the more confidence we'll have that we can overcome obstacles and resolve complications.

When we haven't mastered something relevant to our circumstances, we get the impression that we *lack* control. This impression causes us to feel unprepared, lacking in the requisite skills to achieve success. In this situation, we're more inclined to give up when we face adversity.

For example, suppose you're preparing a report for your boss. It's a complex report, pulling data from multiple spreadsheets. Imagine that you've run into problems. There's evidently something wrong with the formulas you've created to pull the appropriate data.

If you're proficient in the use of spreadsheets, you'll feel comfortable in your ability to investigate and resolve the issue. You'll have a sense of control over your circumstances. Consequently, you'll be inclined to persevere until the matter is resolved. You'll trust yourself to see things through to success.

But let's say you rarely work with spreadsheets. You can input data into cells and create simple formulas, but that's where your expertise ends. In this situation, when you discover complex problems with the report you're creating for your boss, you won't feel in control. You'll likely feel unqualified to investigate and resolve the underlying issues. You'll be more inclined to give up, even if doing so means disappointing your boss.

Herein lies the reason mastery is essential for mental toughness. When we're proficient in something that's relevant to our circumstances, we trust ourselves. We have confidence in our skills and abilities. This confidence reinforces our tenacity and resolve. We perceive ourselves as able to endure the pressure and overcome the obstacles that stand in our path. So we're more likely to press onward than surrender to defeat.

As mentioned above, mastery is always accompanied by boredom. The latter is a natural part of becoming adept at any skill or craft. That being the case, boredom isn't something to avoid.

It's something to *embrace*.

How to Get Comfortable with Boredom

When you feel bored while performing a task, remind yourself why you're performing the task in the first place. What do you hope to accomplish? Why is that outcome important to you?

Let's return to our earlier "spreadsheet" example. You're working with the spreadsheets because your boss assigned the report to you. You hope to produce a report that'll be helpful to him or her. That's important to you because it'll make you look good to your boss. And that positive impression might lead to higher-profile projects, which in turn might lead to a promotion and raise down the road.

You're shifting your attention from the task at hand to your greater goal. This makes it easier to tolerate the boredom you're experiencing in the present. Your attention is focused on your longer-term purpose.

It's also helpful to *acknowledge* that you're bored. Boredom is subtle and often settles in without our realization. Recognize that you're bored and identify the reason (e.g. practicing your craft via repetition is boring). That'll make it easier to accept the boredom and move on before it stirs up negative emotions (stress, frustration, depression, etc.).

Another way to deal with boredom is to turn whatever you're doing into a game. This will make whatever task or project you're working on more enjoyable. You can even attach small rewards to achieving specific milestones.

For example, suppose you're practicing playing scales on the guitar. You know the scales like the back of your hand, so the practice session is boring. Turn the practice session into a game with small rewards. For instance, set a timer for five minutes. Then, try to play the scales up and down without making a single error in form or clarity. If you succeed, enjoy a piece of your favorite candy bar.

Or suppose you're working on the aforementioned spreadsheet report for your boss. It's boring work, particularly if you're adept at using spreadsheets. So, turn it into a game. Set a timer and try to finish a section of the report in the next three minutes. Or come up with a novel strategy for pulling data that you've never employed before.

Another effective tactic is to meditate. Meditation trains your mind to be present. It desensitizes your mind to boredom, encouraging it to find peace and joy in being in the moment. Rather than looking for distractions to stave off boredom, your mind will learn to remain focused and relaxed in the absence of stimulation.

BOREDOM IS a companion to developing mental toughness. It's part of the process. And importantly, far from carrying negative connotations, we should learn to welcome it when it's associated with the skills we practice and hone. After all, it suggests that we're on the cusp of true mastery.

EXERCISE #16

WRITE down the feelings you typically associate with boredom. Some may be positive and some negative. Following are a few examples:

- restlessness
- frustration
- calmness
- satisfaction
- irritability
- amusement
- guilt
- optimism
- pessimism

Next, reframe the negative emotions.

For example, if you typically feel restless when you're bored, determine the reason. Perhaps you were raised to believe that idle time is worthless, and you should always be doing *something*. In this case, you can reframe the idle time as valuable *downtime* during which you have an opportunity to relax and recharge.

Time required: 10 minutes.

HOW TO LEARN THE RIGHT LESSONS FROM FAILURE

~

Failure can be a highly effective teacher. It's also a harsh and unsympathetic one. The insight and value we obtain from it ultimately depend on which lessons we learn.

If we perceive failure to be a scathing judgement on our skills and abilities, we'll eventually learn to dread it. We'll begin to see ourselves as incompetent and inadequate. So pervasive might this dread become in our minds that we'll become unwilling to take risks.

Conversely, if we perceive failure to be nothing more than feedback, we'll recognize it as an opportunity to improve our processes. Rather than feeling incompetent due to our lack of success *this time*, we'll be inclined to incorporate the feedback and try again.

So much depends on how we interpret failure. How we do so will influence our emotions, thoughts, and ultimately our responses. Our perception of failure - and by extension, the lessons we learn from it - can make the difference between giving up and persevering when life becomes difficult.

Consider the following quote from the aforementioned basketball marvel Michael Jordan:

> *I've missed more than 9000 shots in my career. I've lost almost 300 games. Twenty-six times, I've been trusted to take the game-winning shot and missed. I've failed over and over and over*

again in my life. And that is why I succeed."

Another basketball player might have an entirely different reaction if he were to post these numbers. He might even entertain the idea of giving up, convinced that he was a terrible player and unlikely to ever master his craft.

Again, our perception of failure dictates the lessons we learn from it. Seen through the appropriate lens, failure can have a remarkably positive effect on our burgeoning mental toughness.

How Failure Improves Your Mental Toughness

You've likely heard the phrase "that which doesn't kill us makes us stronger." It typically refers to tragedy and misfortune, but it's equally applicable to failure. If we interpret failure as feedback, it toughens us. Each incident further desensitizes us from the crippling emotions that might otherwise surface.

Throughout this process, we become steadily more courageous when we're faced with uncertainty. The idea of making a wrong decision or committing a mistake, and consequently experiencing a negative outcome, holds less and less fear for us. A negative outcome becomes nothing more than feedback, which presents us with an opportunity to learn and improve.

The more prepared we are to interpret failure as feedback rather than a pronouncement of inadequacy, the more courageous we'll become. Eventually, we'll adopt a fearless mindset. We'll notice practical lessons in every negative outcome, an attitude that'll embolden us and reinforce our resilience when we confront setbacks and misfortune.

We discussed the importance of having a growth mindset in the section *How Your Attitude Affects Your Mental Toughness*. Our willingness and readiness to learn from our failures aligns perfectly with this frame of mind. It's an admission that we're imperfect, as well as an acknowledgement that we're capable of learning anything we need in order to persevere and eventually succeed.

This attitude affects every area of our lives. It influences our decisions and actions at school, in the workplace, at home, and with friends and loved ones. It shapes our responses to unexpected obstacles and emotional distress. When we learn the right lessons from failure, we develop greater awareness of ourselves and our capacity to handle pressure and overcome challenges.

5 Lessons to Learn Whenever You "Fail"

So, what *are* the correct lessons that we should learn from failure? How can we ensure that we're taking maximum advantage of the feedback we're presented with? Following are five takeaways that'll reward you as long as you're willing to perceive failure as a stepping stone to improvement and eventual success.

#1 - Success often comes after multiple failures.

Baseball great Babe Ruth was simultaneously known as the Strike Out King and the Home Run King. He once said "every strike brings me closer to the next home run." He recognized that failure wasn't the final outcome. It was merely a milepost on his path to accomplishing something remarkable.

#2 - Each failure provides valuable experience.

Experience has greater value than success. It gives us a healthy perspective regarding our abilities. It also makes us aware of our limitations, highlighting deficits that warrant our attention. Experience is necessary for personal growth.

Every time we fail to achieve our desired outcome, we gain a deeper understanding of the relationship between our decisions and actions and the net result. This knowledge informs our future decisions and actions. We gain awareness and insight and become more effective, all of which make us more tenacious when our results deviate from our expectations.

#3 - Persistence trumps everything.

Inventor Thomas Edison was intimately acquainted with failure. He successfully invented the light bulb after thousands of failed attempts. Edison later said regarding the experience "I haven't failed. I've just found 10,000 ways that won't work."

He understood that persistence in the face of failure is critical to final success. To that end, the refusal to give up is more important than intelligence, talent, and education. Persistence, one of the clearest expressions of mental toughness, trumps everything when failure occurs.

#4 - Fear is unnecessary and unproductive.

Fear prevents us from taking action. And failure is the thing many of us intuitively fear the most. We shudder at the possibility that we'll do something that'll have a negative outcome. We worry that we'll make fools of ourselves. This is the reason it's so difficult to venture outside our comfort zones.

The upside of regularly failing (and possessing the grit to press forward afterward) is that we slowly become desensitized to negative outcomes. We learn that such outcomes are less consequential than we imagine them to be. In short, we come to realize that our fears are overblown.

Once we grow accustomed to failure, perceiving it as an opportunity to learn and improve, the associated fear ceases to have a hold on us. We become more comfortable taking calculated risks to improve our circumstances.

#5 - YOU decide how to feel about failure.

The biggest impediment to our cognitive resilience when we're faced with failure is our emotions. In the section *Mental Toughness and Emotional Mastery*, we talked about emotions in the context of self-awareness, empathy, and self-control. These concepts dovetail with our perception of failure.

We choose how we respond to it. We can choose to embrace the negative emotions that failure stimulates within us (e.g. distress, fear, shame, depression, etc.). Or we can choose to *reframe* failure and assign positive emotions to it. If we interpret failure as an opportunity to learn, we can associate emotions such as interest, hope, inspiration, pride, and even gratitude. These positive emotions help us to embrace optimism about our ongoing personal growth and effectiveness.

ALL OF US grow up fearing failure. The problem is, many of us fail to shed this fear in adulthood. It lies deep in our psyche, dictating our decisions and actions, and preventing us from taking risks, venturing outside our comfort zones, and persevering when life becomes difficult.

When we *reframe* failure, changing our perception of it, we give ourselves an opportunity to take advantage of its attendant insights. This habit reinforces our tenacity when we encounter obstacles, challenges, and other setbacks.

EXERCISE #17

DESCRIBE A SITUATION WHERE YOU FAILED. It doesn't matter whether the failure was big or small, consequential or trivial. Write down what happened and how your decisions or actions (or inaction) led to a negative outcome.

Next, describe the emotions you experienced as a result of that incident.

Did you feel guilty, angry, or discouraged?

Finally, ponder how you might have turned that failure into success.

Here's a personal example to get you started. I taught myself to play the guitar when I was in high school. My early attempts were embarrassing. I couldn't get it right. I failed over and over.

Back then, I often let my emotions get away from me. I'd routinely chastise myself for failing to play well, and feel angry, frustrated, and disappointed all at once. Needless to say, that wasn't conducive to improving my craft.

Eventually, I decided to let go of these negative emotions. I acknowledged them and pressed onward. I committed to getting up at 4:30 a.m. each morning and practicing for hours before heading off to school.

The result? I slowly developed and honed my skill to the point that I was satisfied with it.

Now, it's your turn.

Time required: 15 minutes.

HOW NAVY SEALS DEVELOP MENTAL TOUGHNESS

∼

People who go through the training and selection process to become a United States Navy SEAL are intimately acquainted with the temptation to give up. They endure a difficult 26-week training regimen at Basic Underwater Demolition/SEAL (BUD/S) school. Then, they face a formidable 26-week SEAL Qualification Training course.

The training program is extremely demanding, designed to weed out all but the toughest individuals. Only one in seven enrollees graduate. But despite popular belief, the program doesn't focus on physical superiority. In fact, former Navy SEAL and SEAL Sniper instructor Brandon Webb, reveals a surprising fact about SEAL training. In his book *Red Circle: My Life in the Navy SEAL Sniper Corps and How I Trained*, he notes that "the course is designed for the average athletic male to be able to make it through."

So why do so few enrollees graduate from the program? Webb says in *Red Circle*:

> *What SEAL training really tests is your mental mettle. It is designed to to push you mentally to the brink, over and over again, until you are hardened and able to take on any task with confidence, regardless of the odds - or until you break."*

There's a lot we can learn about mental toughness from Navy SEALS.

This section will examine their psychological resolve and explore the practical tactics they use to deal with adversity in the field.

Mental Toughness Trumps Physical Toughness

Navy SEALS undoubtedly need to be physically fit to handle the challenges associated with their jobs. Theirs is a demanding profession. While, as Webb suggests, the average athletic male can pass the training program's physical fitness test, graduates routinely work out to stay in top physical shape.

But the *mental* training takes priority.

Navy SEALS are often placed in hostile and extreme situations that trigger a natural fear response. In these situations, there's a risk they'll become overwhelmed with the emotions associated with this fear. They undergo psychological conditioning designed to desensitize themselves to it.

Many people believe Navy SEALs to be fearless. But this is a misconception. SEALs experience fear just like all of us. The difference is, they've learned to control it so they're able to press onward and complete their missions. This is possible due to a mental training strategy known as habituation.

Habituation involves repeated exposure to stimulus that triggers an undesirable response (in this case, fear). Frequent exposure acclimates the individual to the stimulus, thereby diminishing the unwanted response. Through this training, Navy SEALs learn to conquer and control their fears so they can do their jobs.

Notice that SEALs' mental toughness, and their training that helps to develop it, doesn't preclude fear. It helps SEALs to *master* it so that the fear doesn't control them, which would limit their operational effectiveness in life-threatening situations.

Let's now take a look at some to the training tactics used by Navy SEALs to strengthen their mental fortitude and psychological preparedness.

5 Tactics Used by Navy Seals to Deal with Adversity

The training techniques employed by Navy SEALs are immediately applicable. The focus isn't on theory. It's on practical application. Below, I'll share five techniques as described by former and current SEALs, and explain how you can apply them in your daily experience.

#1 - Practice positive self-talk.

Part of the BUD/S training program involves staying underwater with breathing gear. This is known as "pool comp." While the trainee is underwater, his instructor will break his breathing equipment. The trainee must remain calm and fix the problem. Positive self-talk is essential to keeping panic at bay and completing this test successfully.

Application: Whenever you feel overwhelmed, whether at your job or at home, remind yourself that your skills, abilities, and knowledge will help you to prevail. Tell yourself to remain calm and relaxed. Tell yourself that your current circumstances are temporary, and will dissipate when you give them attention.

#2 - Continue training after you master something.

Navy SEALs must master a wide variety of disciplines. The problem is, most of their time isn't spent in the field where they can put these skills to use. SEALs experience a lot of downtime. If they neglect to constantly practice their skills, they'll get rusty. So they train over and over, guaranteeing they'll be ready to perform when they're on deployment.

Application: Keep practicing skills that are essential to your long-term success, even if you feel you've mastered them. Try to use them each day to ensure they stay sharp. For example, writing is obviously a major part of being an author. But it's tempting to take significant time off between books. Many authors, myself included, resist this temptation and write every day to keep our writing "muscles" in tiptop shape.

#3 - Focus on small wins.

Like most of us, Navy SEALs set goals for themselves. But their goals do little to help them endure the mental punishment associated with their jobs. To stay mentally strong and achieve their goals, they practice "segmentation." They break down their larger goals into *micro* goals. For example, rather than focusing on completing a 20-mile run, they focus on reaching the tree they see in their path in the distance. Once they reach the tree, they focus on scaling a hill that's within sight. And so on until they complete their run.

Application: Break down intimidating projects into small steps. Ideally, these steps can be completed within a single day. For example, suppose you've been tasked with giving a presentation at your workplace. Segment the project. Write down each step, including selecting a topic, writing the content, preparing slides, and brainstorming questions for your audience. You can further segment writing the content into creating your introduction, the body of your presentation, and your conclusion.

#4 - Visualize your desired outcome.

This is something that Navy SEALs and world-class athletes (e.g. Olympians) have in common. They mentally rehearse their activities and visualize their success. This technique is effective because, according to psychologists, the brain doesn't differentiate between actual experiences and imagined experiences. Because of this cognitive quirk, visualization prepares our minds for success and squelches our fears in the process.

Application: If you're worried about something you need to do, visualize doing it successfully. For example, suppose you're concerned about a big presentation you're expected to give at your workplace. Close your eyes and see yourself giving the presentation. Take yourself through each step, each part of your speech, and each slide. Visualize completing your presentation and responding confidently to the audience's questions. See yourself in the ideal state you hope to experience.

#5 - Anticipate everything that might go wrong.

A large part of a Navy SEAL's mental conditioning is to control the innate fear that surfaces in the face of adversity. For most of us, adverse circumstances are unpleasant and frustrating. For SEALs, such circumstances can be deadly.

To combat this fear, SEALs rehearse relentlessly, trying to anticipate every problem that might prevent them from completing their missions. Before Navy SEAL Team Six descended upon Osama bin Laden's compound in May 2011, they created a life-sized model of his compound. They then spent three weeks training for the operation. During this intense training, they brainstormed and simulated unexpected complications and rehearsed their responses to them.

Application: If you're working on a project and worried that something might go wrong, ponder the difficulties you might experience. Let's again suppose you're planning to give a presentation. The audiovisual equipment you're using to display slides might malfunction. What will you do if that happens? You might forget a piece of your speech. How will you recover? Someone in your audience might ask a question for which you lack an answer. How will you respond to this individual? Try to anticipate every possible complication, and then rehearse your responses. You'll feel more comfortable and confident that you'll be able to handle any problem that surfaces.

NAVY SEALS MUST BE MENTALLY tough in order to overcome their fears and do their jobs effectively. We can use many aspects of their training to develop our own mental toughness. The tactics they use to ensure their operational effectiveness can help us to deal with adversity, uncertainty, and misfortune in our daily lives.

EXERCISE #18

∽

WRITE down three incidents during which you were paralyzed by fear, lack of confidence, and negative self-talk, and thereby unable to take purposeful action. Describe how you would resolve each of these three situations *today* using the mental conditioning tactics favored by Navy SEALs.

Time required: 10 minutes.

PART III

A QUICK-START GUIDE TO BECOMING MENTALLY TOUGH

∼

We've covered a lot of material. Along with the exercises found in each section of this book, all of it is important if you wish to develop mental toughness. But admittedly, it's a lot to digest. And when you're faced with a mountain of tips, tactics, and strategies (and exercises!), it can feel overwhelming.

It's like visiting your favorite buffet and being spellbound by all of the delicious food on offer. Where do you start? How do you take full advantage?

Part III will help you to get started. First, we'll take a look at several real-life applications of mental toughness. This will further distance the idea of mental strength from the theoretical and instead highlight it as applied psychology. Something that's experiential, less abstract and more focused on real-world results.

Second, I'll take you through a simple 10-step regimen designed to kick-start your training. This program prioritizes the fundamentals. It's a primer. As you progress, you'll no doubt want to expand the regimen to fit your circumstances.

Finally, you'll learn how to maintain your mental toughness once you've started to develop it. Everything we've discussed in this book, from emotional mastery to psychological preparedness, combines to form something like a muscle. It's like any muscle. The more you use it the stronger it grows. The less you use it the faster it atrophies. I'll share several strategies that'll help to ensure your mental toughness "muscles" continue to develop.

Enough chatter. We're nearing the finish line. Let's put everything we've covered thus far to use.

PRACTICAL APPLICATIONS OF MENTAL TOUGHNESS

~

Mental toughness makes sense on a conceptual level. But the conversation can easily become academic, never reaching the point where it takes on legitimate, real-life substance and gravity. In this way, talking about mental toughness is similar to discussing how to be courageous and confident, more self-aware, more charismatic, and less introverted. As a self-improvement goal, it remains ethereal - and its value hypothetical - until we know how to apply it in our daily lives.

This section addresses that gap. Below, we'll explore how being mentally strong in difficult situations can pay dividends in various areas of your life. I'll use examples to illustrate the many forms mental toughness can take and describe how you might benefit from its application.

Some of the examples may seem trivial to you. But that's partly the aim of this section: to demonstrate the countless small ways mental toughness can prove beneficial. To that end, what follows is merely a jumping-off point. You'll undoubtedly think of many ways to apply tenacity, impulse control, emotional strength, and psychological readiness that are unique to your circumstances.

Let's start with our home lives.

Mental Toughness at Home

When we think of being at home, we imagine feeling comfortable and relaxed. But of course, difficult situations can surface at home just like anywhere else. We don't control everything that happens to us, and thus we're often forced to deal with situations that test our patience and resolve.

For example, if you have a young child at home, you're well-acquainted with the frustration that can often arise. Or suppose you're unable to find a cherished heirloom, and discover (with shock) that a family member unwittingly discarded it. Or let's say you're trying to focus on reading a book, but construction workers nearby are making so much noise that it's all but impossible to focus.

These situations can trigger a host of negative emotions that can lead to unhealthy and unrewarding escalation. Being mentally tough entails keeping these emotions in check. It involves enduring the stress and adapting to your circumstances, as unpleasant as they might be.

Mental Toughness in the Workplace

The workplace can be a hotbed of frustration, distress, and disappointment. Consider that you interact with a variety of people every day. Not only does each person possess unique personality quirks, but their moods can shift according to their individual circumstances. It can be a virtual minefield.

Additionally, you might experience setbacks such as failing to make deadlines, missing your sales quotas, and being passed up for expected promotions. And then there are the office politics, where rewards and punishments, both subtle and overt, are doled out based on who's currently in and out of favor.

Keeping your emotions in check is critical to staying sane in this type of an environment. It's also important to silence your inner critic (your coworkers will happily fill that role), keep a positive outlook, and celebrate your small victories. Remember, mental toughness comes from within you. It has nothing to do with receiving validation from others.

Mental Toughness as a Freelancer

If you're a freelancer, you're no stranger to challenges, setbacks, and other difficult situations. From working with grumpy clients and pursuing unpaid invoices to feeling inadequate, incompetent, and untalented when compared to your competition, freelancing is a tough road. Being successful requires a tough mind.

An emotionally fragile freelancer will always struggle to feel comfortable with his business. This person will continually question his abilities while feeling like an amateur. This self-doubt can be an extremely frustrating predicament, particularly when clients complain, request an endless string of revisions, and are late to pay invoices.

The mentally tough freelancer will be better equipped to take these difficulties in stride. She'll be able to work productively with irritable clients; she'll respond professionally to requests for revisions; and she'll display confidence when following up on late invoices.

Mental toughness may be a freelancer's best friend.

Mental Toughness in School

We rarely think of school as an environment that requires mental toughness. But in fact, school can be just as much of a breeding ground for distress, disappointment, anxiety, and despair as the workplace. Moreover, the social dynamics of a school can turn it into just as much of a snake pit.

What role does mental toughness play in such an environment?

Studying for exams when you'd rather catch up on sleep calls for impulse control. Dealing with a terrible grade on a project in which you invested significant time and effort demands emotional control. Completing assignments on time when life conspires against you makes a positive mindset an indispensable asset.

In some ways, school can impose more psychological pressure than the workplace. Mental toughness helps students manage stress, adapt to adverse situations, and even become less emotionally vulnerable to bullying.

Mental Toughness in Competitive Sports

If you participate in competitive sports, you already know how mental toughness (or lack thereof) influences your performance. But it's worth highlighting a few examples to drive the point home.

During practice sessions, your body and mind can become exhausted to the point that you want to give up. It's your grit and resolve that keep you going, compelling you to press onward when it feels like you have nothing left in the tank.

While competing, you might experience self-doubt. You'll question yourself and your abilities. Are you truly as good as your competition? Are they better than you? Faster? Bigger? Stronger? As these questions surface, you'll begin to feel anxious and unfocused. You might even feel inferior to your competition.

Mental toughness will help you to concentrate on your performance and remain calm. Visualizing your success will help to quell your self-doubt. And having confidence in your abilities, which spring from your hard work, will extinguish the psychological pressure. A mentally-tough athlete believes in herself, stays positive, deconstructs negative self-talk, and performs well despite the obstacles she encounters.

Mental Toughness and Your Goals

Setting personal goals is important because goals give us purpose. They help us to focus on things we want to accomplish. They give us direction as they provide us with a destination. This direction helps us make better decisions and take more purposeful action.

The problem is, the effort required to achieve our goals often runs contrary to our impulses. For example, suppose your goal is to exercise at the gym five days a week. There will be times when you'll be tempted to forgo your workout and spend that time on your couch watching your favorite show on Netflix.

Suppose your goal is to lose 20 lbs. You decide to stay away from junk food. If you've ever tried to give up sugar (and who among us hasn't tried?), you know firsthand how strong the cravings can be.

Suppose your goal is to meet three new people a day. But let's say you're an introvert and introducing yourself to strangers is a scary proposition. You'll occasionally be tempted to abandon your goal and retreat to your comfort zone.

In each of these scenarios, mental toughness will reinforce your resolve when the cravings and temptations surface. In fact, a large part of achieving *any* goal is psychological in nature; success relies on our ability to resist our impulses. Mental strength in the form of tenacity, discipline, and emotional mastery is necessary for us to exert impulse control.

MENTAL TOUGHNESS IS crucial when dealing with life's major hardships, such as divorce, the loss of a job, or the death of a loved one. But it's also useful to think of mental toughness in the context of how you can apply it to deal constructively with life's *smaller* complications. These are the situations that occur throughout the day. While they're smaller in consequence, they add up and can exert enormous cumulative pressure on us.

Let's now go through a simple 10-step mental toughness training program. It'll ensure you get started on the right foot, laying the foundation for ongoing development down the road.

A 10-STEP TRAINING PROGRAM FOR TOUGHENING YOUR MIND

∽

It's one thing to *talk* (or read) about developing mental toughness. It's another thing to actually do it. This subject matter is so comprehensive and has such huge ramifications that it's tough to know where to get started.

In this section, I'll give you a simple, quick-start action plan. We'll go through 10 steps, each of which focuses on an important principle of mental toughness. Note that what follows is far from a complete, encyclopedic initiative on toughening your mind. Rather, it's designed to give you a jumpstart in the right direction. The fact is, it'd be impossible for me to create an all-inclusive program for you as developing mental toughness becomes a personal journey once you master the basics.

So let's start developing the skills and knowledge you'll need to deal effectively with the challenges, complications, and stressors life inevitably throws at you.

Step 1: Contemplate how you can apply mental toughness in your life.

The key to starting off right is to stop thinking about mental toughness as an abstract idea and *start* thinking about it as something that has real-life value to you. In the previous section, we explored some of its myriad practical applications. Here, consider how you'll apply your newly-toughened mindset to your personal circumstances.

Our goals and aspirations become easier to achieve once we identify our purpose for achieving them. So ask yourself *why* you'd like to develop mental resilience. How will it improve your life? For example, will it help you to resist junk food while dieting? Will it give you the discipline to exercise daily? Will it provide you the emotional strength you'll need to handle the impending loss of a dearly-loved family member?

Developing mental toughness is a difficult endeavor. Knowing your purpose will help you to persevere when you struggle.

Step 2: Segment your goals.

You're no stranger to setting goals. The fact that you're reading this book means self-improvement is important to you, and it's difficult to improve yourself without goals.

Having said that, *setting* goals isn't enough. Nor is even setting the *right* goals. The key is to break down your goals into easily-manageable steps. In the section *How Navy SEALs Develop Mental Toughness*, we talked about the practice of segmentation. Navy SEALs use this technique to endure the mental stress and pressure that accompany their jobs. They use it to avoid becoming overwhelmed.

This is the same technique used by distance runners when they participate in marathons. When they're exhausted, both physically and mentally, they don't focus on the finish line. They focus on the next point within sight. Once they reach that point, they focus on the *next* point within sight. They do this over and over, confident they'll eventually reach the finish line.

Segment your own goals to resist the temptation to give up when the going gets tough.

Step 3: Reframe difficult situations as opportunities to improve.

Building mental strength depends on how we think of our circumstances. If we perceive adversity and misfortune to be hardships that leave us powerless victims, we'll be more inclined to lose heart and surrender. Conversely, if we perceive them to be learning opportunities, we'll be more likely to consider their positive aspects. It's a matter of reframing how we interpret challenging scenarios.

For example, suppose you're a freelancer discussing a project with a potential client. The client ends up balking, rejecting your proposal outright. In this scenario, if you habitually consider yourself the victim in negative situations, you may instinctively question your abilities and skills. If this outcome happens repeatedly, you might even begin to think of yourself as worthless, and be tempted to close down your business.

But suppose you framed this client's rejection in a positive light. For example, you might interpret it as a reinforcement of your pricing structure (i.e. charging higher fees leads to better clients). You may perceive it as an affirmation of your principles (i.e. the type of work you're willing or unwilling to do). By reframing difficult situations, you get to choose the insight you infer from them. This shift in mindset can make the difference between falling into despair when things go wrong and feeling inspired to persist.

Step 4: Practice controlling negative emotions.

Emotional intelligence is a massive topic that touches on numerous disciplines and subject areas, such as empathy, self-awareness, and self-regulation. Such matters lie beyond the scope of this discussion. But we can still benefit from exploring how to get our emotions under control without getting lost in the weeds in the process.

As we discussed in the section *Mental Toughness and Emotional Mastery*, negative emotions are natural. In fact, they can be highly useful in focusing our attention and spurring us to improve ourselves. The problem is, emotions like anxiety, anger, and fear can overwhelm us and paralyze us into inaction. A little goes a long way, and too much can quickly overload us.

We shouldn't suppress negative emotions. On the contrary, we should learn to *manage* them. The best way to do this is to question whether your feelings align with logic and reason. When they're in sync, it's much easier to take purposeful action and make good decisions when things go wrong.

For example, suppose your retirement portfolio takes a beating in the market. It's down 25%. You're angry and worried that your investments will no longer sufficiently fund your retirement. Stop. Take a breath. Now ask yourself whether these negative emotions align with reason. We know from history that the market typically rallies soon after it contracts. Protracted downswings (i.e. bear markets) that last longer than a couple of years are rare.

Armed with this knowledge, it becomes easier to manage your anger and worry. Rather than letting them paralyze you, you can make good decisions and take sensible action (e.g. Reallocating your investments to more promising sectors). In this example, your anger and worry *inform* your decisions. They *prompt* you to take action rather than incapacitating you.

It's not always easy to control negative emotions. But the more consistent you are in using this technique, the easier it becomes.

Step 5: Visualize your performance.

This step is both easy and simple. Here's how to do it: whenever you're about to do something, close your eyes and see yourself doing it perfectly in your mind. Then, imagine how you'll respond to various challenges.

Rehearsing your performance in your head does two important things. First, it trains your mind to expect success. In his book *The Young Champion's Mind*, Jim Afremow notes the following:

> *... the brain does not always differentiate between real and vividly imagined experiences because the same systems in the brain are deployed for both types of experiences."*

When you visualize doing something successfully, your brain thinks it's real. Consequently, visualization can literally improve your chances of success. This is the reason world-class athletes use this technique before they compete. If it works for them, it'll work for you.

The second thing mental rehearsal does is prepare you for every possible contingency. When you visualize how you'll respond to various challenges, you train your mind to react faster. Rather than being forced to interpret each setback in the moment and choose the appropriate response, your responses will already be in place. You'll spend less time ruminating about your situation, and find it easier to "get back in the game" when you confront obstacles.

Step 6: Manage your inner critic.

Like negative emotions, your inner critic can be your friend or your enemy. Much depends on how much control you exert over it. (For a broader discussion of this negative voice in your head, including useful tactics for taming it, see the section *Mental Toughness and Your Inner Critic*.)

One of your inner critic's superpowers is catastrophic thinking. It assumes the worst will happen in every situation. This outlook is contrary to logic and reason, and counters our intention to press on when we confront adversity.

For example, suppose you're trying to stay away from sugary foods. One day, you give into temptation and eat a donut. Your inner critic will try to convince you that this single mistake will have disastrous consequences. It will tell you that you'll never be able to stick to a healthy diet, and you'll inevitably become morbidly obese and pitifully lazy. You'll be the laughing stock of everyone around you. And worst of all, you'll have proven that you're destined for failure.

Your inner critic can be a jerk.

You can learn to control this internal negative monologue by practicing positive self-talk. This doesn't mean telling yourself things that are untrue. Rather, it involves positive thought management. This includes affirming your strengths, acknowledging your weaknesses, and recognizing your ability to improve the latter at will. Over time, your inner critic will find itself without an audience.

Step 7: Get rid of "emotional icebergs."

Emotional icebergs are personal beliefs regarding how we see ourselves, how we think others should act around us, and our place in the world. We're only partially aware of these icebergs. Like real ones, most of their "mass" sits under the surface with only their tips visible above it. Consequently, we often fail to recognize them even as they work against us.

Following are a few examples of emotional icebergs:

- "Everything I do should be perfect."
- "Life should be fair."
- "If I fail, it's because I'm a failure."
- "Showing my feelings is a sign of weakness."
- "My parents should thank me when I do something for them."
- "My coworkers should respect me."
- "I should always avoid conflict."

Emotional icebergs are insidious. They're cunning and subtle, slowly chipping away at our resolve, grit, and impulse control beyond our notice. Worse, many of them stem from childhood, and are therefore deeply ingrained in our psyche.

But we can get rid of them. The "secret" is to challenge them, just as you might challenge your inner critic whenever it makes ridiculous claims. The next time you notice yourself instinctively responding to a challenging situation in an unhealthy manner, stop and investigate the reason.

For example, suppose you've unintentionally angered someone and have rushed to smooth things over. Your top priority is to ensure they're no longer angry with you. Stop and ask yourself why you've acted in this manner. Is it because you believe everyone should be happy with you at all times (a common emotional iceberg)? If so, ask yourself whether this personal belief is true. Might it be unreasonable?

By consistently challenging our emotional icebergs, we can gradually melt them and thereby make them less formidable.

Step 8: Practice recovering after setbacks and failure.

Have you ever witnessed someone immediately getting back in the saddle after he or she suffers misfortune? They make it look easy. You might have found yourself wondering how this person does it.

Chances are, he or she has had a lot of practice. Therein lies a valuable lesson with regard to developing mental toughness.

None of us are born knowing how to recover after setbacks. It's not intuitive. It's something we learn. We discover from experience that failures are seldom disastrous or final. When we stumble, we pick ourselves up, dust ourselves off, and continue onward.

The more we do it, the easier it becomes.

The key to quickly recovering from failure is twofold. First, we need to immediately confront and dispute our negative thoughts regarding it. Second, we need to reengage the part of our mind that recognizes our abilities, creativity, and self-worth.

For example, suppose you've given a presentation at your job that goes poorly. If you're highly susceptible to negative thoughts, you might wilt under the self-recrimination. You may decide you're incompetent, unprofessional, and pathetically unqualified to instruct or inform others. And so you may resolve to never again give a presentation.

But let's say you have an entirely different mindset regarding failure. When negative thoughts surface, you immediately dispute them because you know they're untrue. Then, you remind yourself that you're highly skilled, knowledgeable, creative, and resourceful. In this light, you're able to quickly rebound from this setback. And once you figure out why your presentation failed, you'll feel certain that your *next* presentation will be a success.

The more practice you get in recovering from setbacks, the less dejected you'll feel after experiencing them. You'll eventually find that dusting yourself off and getting back in the saddle becomes instinctive.

Step 9: Build habits that encourage discipline and grit.

We know from our discussion in the section *The Role of Willpower and Motivation* that both are unreliable resources. We can count on neither when we need to persevere through discomfort and hardship. A better strategy is to form habits and routines that reinforce our resolve.

Have you ever lay in bed, awake minutes before your alarm is set to go off, yet unable to escape the warm covers? Then, your alarm sounds and you finally get out of bed. The alarm is a trigger that starts your morning routine of brushing your teeth, taking a shower, getting dressed, and drinking coffee. This routine is a sequence of habits. It occurs naturally, even though you found it difficult to do the first unpleasant action (getting out of bed).

As noted in the section *Mental Toughness and Your Habits*, our habits are more reliable than willpower and motivation when we need to overcome obstacles. They keep us on track, helping us to control our impulses. They help us to delay gratification, focusing our attention on the challenges in front of us rather than allowing us to give in to temptation.

For example, suppose you aspire to go for a jog each evening after returning home from work. If you've had a long, trying day, you'll be tempted to relax on your couch and watch television. But let's say you've adopted the habit of donning your running clothes (sneakers, shorts, and t-shirt) immediately after returning home each evening. This habit is so deeply ingrained that it now occurs naturally. With this habit in place, you'll be better able to resist your couch and TV, and actually go for your evening jog.

Our habits make it easier to persevere when we encounter challenges and complications. Adopt good habits, and you'll be less inclined to give up when you feel uncomfortable or under pressure.

Step 10: Celebrate the small victories.

We tend to focus on final results. For example, in college we define success in the context of our GPA. When it comes to our careers, we define success on whether we get the promotions we desire. If we're trying to lose a certain amount of weight, we focus on whether we reach our final target weight.

Our focus on the final outcome is admirable, but it often comes at the cost of ignoring the smaller successes along the way. These successes are an important component in training our minds to keep going when we experience setbacks.

For example, suppose you're dieting and exercising in order to lose 30 lbs. Losing this amount of weight is a formidable endeavor, and it consumes your attention. If you stumble along the way (e.g. you eat a candy bar or you neglect to exercise one day), you may feel so disappointed in yourself that you're tempted to give up. Your focus is on the "finish line," and it's such a long ways off that it feels impossible to achieve in light of your misstep.

But let's say you take the time to celebrate the small victories. You compliment yourself on visiting the gym four days a week. You reward yourself (e.g. renting a movie you've wanted to watch) for eating healthy over the past three days. You give yourself permission to watch one episode of your favorite sitcom for successfully resisting the urge to eat junk food *today*.

Celebrating the small victories makes us feel good about whatever we're trying to achieve. It makes us happy. And this repeated feeling of happiness can motivate us to stick to our guns when we're uncomfortable - physically and emotionally - down the road.

YOU NOW HAVE AN ACTION PLAN. Ten steps to get you started in toughening your mind, and in the process building your grit, tenacity, and resolve whenever you face discomfort and distress.

What's next? Once you've developed mental toughness, the challenge then becomes maintaining it. If your life is without regular setbacks, obstacles, and misfortune, your newly-toughened mind can atrophy, like any muscle. We'll solve this issue in the next section.

THE MENTAL TOUGHNESS MAINTENANCE GUIDE

∼

A large part of developing mental toughness involves cognitive restructuring. This is a process during which you question all of the negative, inaccurate thoughts, attitudes, and emotions you harbor. It's about changing how you view the world as well as your place in it. Rather than accepting your automatic reactions to your circumstances and trusting them as reasonable, you put them under the microscope and scrutinize them.

Cognitive restructuring isn't a once-and-done process, at least not in the context of maintaining mental toughness. It's something you'll (hopefully) attend to on a continual basis, regularly monitoring your thoughts and stress testing them for validity.

Life sometimes grants us periods during which we suffer no major setbacks or misfortune. Everything goes right for us. The problem is, mental toughness is like a muscle. It atrophies if we neglect to make use of it. Fortunately, we can easily prevent this from happening by performing a simple mental workout regimen. The following eight exercises are designed to help you stay mentally strong during times when life is free of psychological and emotional stress.

8 Exercises to Maintain and Reinforce Your Mental Toughness

These exercises may seem inconsequential. All of them are easy, simple, and require little time. But don't underestimate their collective impact. If you perform them each day, they'll have a considerable influence on how you process your thoughts and emotions.

#1 - **Practice simple meditation.**

We're not talking about sitting with crystals, uttering mantras, or strengthening your root chakra. Here, we just want to sit for a few minutes with our eyes closed and focus on our breathing. We want to be present in the moment.

Simple meditation allows us to disconnect from the world, giving us a brief respite from all its deadlines, expectations, and other stressors. It gives us a chance to catch our breath.

Science supports the practice as it relates to brain functioning consistent with mental toughness. Studies have shown that meditation triggers increased activity in the anterior cingulate cortex (ACC).[1] This is an area of the brain that contributes to attention regulation, decision-making, impulse control, and emotional responses.

You can practice simple meditation anywhere and at any time. All you need is a bit of privacy and five minutes. If it's noisy in your surroundings, don a cheap set of headphones.

#2 - Ask yourself "What's the worst that can happen?"

Even when life is good and everything is going right, self-doubt can creep in. You'll begin to second-guess your decisions and hesitate before acting in fear that you'll make mistakes.

Self-doubt is a natural and healthy part of our psychology. It helps us to make good decisions, encourages us to do our best work, and protects us from negative outcomes. The problem is, it can also paralyze us. It can consume our thoughts, promoting fear and indecision, thereby becoming a liability.

This exercise counters this effect. When you find yourself in doubt, vacillating rather than taking action, ask yourself *"What's the worst that can happen if I do XYZ?"* The answer will reveal that mistakes are rarely disastrous. It reminds us that we can take action without fear, confident that doing so won't lead to catastrophe. The more often we do this, the less we'll hesitate when faced with uncertainty.

#3 - Get comfortable with taking risks.

Taking risks exposes us to the possibility of failure. And that can be an unsettling feeling. But failure is nothing to fear. While there's usually a price to pay, the price is seldom ruinous. Meanwhile, taking risks gives us valuable experience as well as an opportunity to enjoy a specific reward. We take risks to produce a desired outcome.

A part of cognitive restructuring involves adjusting how we think about failure. Rather than perceiving it to be something to avoid at all costs, we should learn to accept it as an ever-present hazard of taking action. In fact, we should learn to *anticipate* it. The upside is that we stand to gain valuable insight from failure. We learn what works and what doesn't.

Take small risks throughout the day.

For example, suppose you're visiting a favorite restaurant. Order a meal you've never tried in the past. If you're at the gym, try a new machine. If you're with a friend, be open in a way that may seem odd to you (e.g. express your appreciation for his or her friendship). The practice of taking small risks exposes you to failure without major consequence. Along the way, your mind will gradually stop fearing failure, and instead treat it as an opportunity to learn and improve.

#4 - Practice ignoring things that are beyond your control.

The Stoics had this correct. Some things lay beyond our control and therefore shouldn't consume our attentional resources. Epictetus, a Greek philosopher who died in 135 AD, noted the following in his *Discourses*:

> *The chief task in life is simply this: to identify and separate matters so that I can say clearly to myself which are externals not under my control, and which have to do with the choices I actually control."*

Epictetus was a smart man.

Spending time and attention on things we're unable to control or influence is a waste of energy. Ignoring such things only benefits us. It frees our mind space so we can focus on things that we can actually change.

Try the following:

The next time you read something online - e.g. anything regarding politics or dismal current events - ask yourself *"How much control do I have over this?"* If the answer is "none," ignore it and move on. You'll reduce your stress, conserve energy to allocate toward things you can change, and probably sleep better in the process. Moreover, you'll find it easier to control your emotions, an important component of mental toughness.

#5 - When your willpower wanes, focus on your purpose.

There are undoubtedly tasks on your to-do list that you'd like to postpone or avoid entirely. When we're faced with such tasks, it's sometimes difficult to summon the mental fortitude to attend to them. They may be unpleasant. Or they may require us to abandon (even if only temporarily) a more gratifying activity. During these times, focus on why the task needs to be completed.

For example, suppose you need to finish an important project at your workplace. You expect doing so will require three hours. You're not looking forward to it, and you'd rather spend the time surfing the internet. Remind yourself *why* you need to complete the project. Did your boss give you a concrete deadline? Will you be unable to participate in another project if you fail to finish this one? Are your coworkers counting on you to finish on time?

This simple mental exercise can spur you to action when you otherwise lack the willpower. By focusing on your purpose - i.e. on your *why* - you'll spark the motivation you need to act.

Here's a silly, but illustrative, example from my own life:

When I was in high school, there was a girl in my class who I wanted to impress. I knew she played rock guitar. Like any young man in that situation, I decided to become a guitar virtuoso to dazzle her. So I practiced relentlessly, getting up at 4:30 a.m. each day. There were many mornings when I wanted to stay in bed. But I'd remind myself of my *why*. And immediately after doing so, I'd tear the covers off, grab my guitar, and get to work.

It's amazing what you can convince yourself to do when you focus on your purpose.

#6 - **Replace your inner critic with an inner optimist.**

Your inner critic is a natural pessimist. Every claim it makes is cynical and bleak. And when it's feeling particular unkind, it can be downright disparaging. Following are some of the dubious claims my inner critic enjoys tossing my way:

- "You're not smart enough."
- "You're ugly."
- "You're fat."
- "No one cares about you."
- "You mess everything up."

Sound familiar? Again, mean-spirited. And completely unproductive.

We talked at length about how to silence this obnoxious internal voice in the section *Mental Toughness and Your Inner Critic*. Here, we're going to take things one step further. We're going to replace this voice with an inner optimist.

One of the core tactics we discussed with regard to silencing your inner critic is to always ask for evidence of its uncharitable claims. For example, if your inner critic says *"no one cares about you,"* you should rightfully respond with *"prove it."* This alone will put a muzzle on your inner critic.

But let's go one step further. In this example, remind yourself of all the people in your life who do indeed care deeply for you. Think of family members, friends, and even coworkers with whom you've worked for years. They care about you because you're a good person. You're trustworthy, fair, and responsible. Maybe you're also compassionate, funny, and quick to forgive. The point is, people care about you because they enjoy being around you.

This is an example of replacing your inner pessimist with an inner optimist. Doing so will influence how you view yourself, including your capacity to have a positive impact on the world around you.

#7 - Regularly venture outside your comfort zone.

We tend to stick to things that are familiar to us. We visit the same restaurants over and over. We participate in the same activities with our friends whenever we spend time with them. We even stay in unhealthy relationships, largely because we know what to expect. Uncertainty is always uncomfortable, and most of us try to avoid that feeling whenever possible.

The problem is, staying inside our comfort zone insulates us from experiences that may hold valuable lessons. If we never try new things nor take calculated risks, we rob ourselves of the opportunity to grow. If we continually cocoon ourselves from uncertainty, we never give ourselves a chance to truly develop mental toughness, tempered by life's unplanned complications.

Even *after* we develop mental toughness, it's easy to fall back into this bad habit. No one relishes feeling uncomfortable or exposed to uncertainty. We naturally favor predictability. It poses less risk to us.

That's a problem when it comes to maintaining your newly-toughened mindset. As noted above, mental toughness is like a muscle that needs regular exercise.

I recommend you look for opportunities to do small things that lie outside your comfort zone. Get used to the discomfort that accompanies uncertainty. You'll train your mind that trying unfamiliar things won't result in disaster. On the contrary, new experiences can broaden your skill set, improve your problem-solving ability, and boost your confidence that you can overcome any obstacles you encounter.

#8 - Test your ability to master new skills.

Venturing outside your comfort zone can (and should) take the form of learning new skills. By doing so, you train your mind that nothing is beyond your capacity to learn, and even master with time. This acknowledgement will reinforce your mental toughness, preventing atrophy when times are good and absent of stress.

For example, suppose you've never prepared a meal. The idea of starting with raw ingredients and cooking something edible is intimidating to you. This feeling is directly connected to your lack of familiarity working in the kitchen.

Now, let's say you decide to venture outside your comfort zone in this area. You're committed to cooking dinner for yourself. You do so, and lo and behold the meal isn't bad. In fact, it's quite good. So, you do it again the following night. And again the night after that. The more you do it, the better you get. Eventually, you become skilled in the kitchen.

This process involves desensitization. It gives you a chance to confront your fears through repeated exposure. Along the way, it allows you to master something that once seemed daunting to you. The result? Not only will you have acquired a new skill, but you'll have also boosted your confidence that you can learn practically anything. This belief in yourself will reinforce your resolve whenever you face adversity and unfamiliar circumstances.

MAINTAINING mental toughness is just as important as developing it in the first place. It's a frame of mind that will benefit you in every area of your life. That being so, it'd be a tragedy to let this "muscle" waste away from nonuse, especially after the hard work you put in to develop it.

These exercises are designed to help keep this muscle strong. As long as it remains so, you'll be able to rely on it whenever life presents you with unanticipated challenges and obstacles.

---

[1] Hölzel B.K.; Ott U.; Hempel H.; Hackl A.; Wolf K.; Stark R.; Vaitl D. (2007). "Differential engagement of anterior cingulate cortex and adjacent medial frontal cortex in adept meditators and nonmeditators". Neuroscience Letters.

FINAL THOUGHTS ON DEVELOPING MENTAL TOUGHNESS

∼

All of us encounter setbacks and misfortune. They're inevitable. What matters is how we respond to them.

We don't control most of what happens to us during any given day. We can plan how we *want* things to progress, create exhaustive to-do lists, and even rehearse how we'll respond to potential issues. But ultimately, we're flying blind.

When life throws us a curve ball, a predicament that deviates from our plans, we're left with two options: adapt with resolve or react with emotion. Top performers in every area of life choose the former.

It's not easy. No one is born with innate resolve. No one is gifted at birth with emotional mastery and psychological resilience. We learn these things by experiencing obstacles, pressure, and distress. Just as steel is tempered in fire, our minds are tempered by adversity. We're toughened by hardship and discomfort.

The goal of *The Mental Toughness Handbook* has been to streamline, and thereby optimize, this process. Rather than letting life's unpredictable curve balls dictate the growth of your mental toughness, you've chosen to control your progress. You've opted to steer your own ship.

And that's something to celebrate.

Many people believe themselves to be mentally tough, but lack the grit and tenacity that define this state of mind. Many others talk about *becoming* mentally tough - and they even buy a book or two on doing so - but never take the first step. Oftentimes, the books they've purchased remain unread on their shelves (or on their phones and e-readers).

You're different. You've read this book and (hopefully) done the exercises. You're committed to your personal growth in this critical area. And if you continue to apply the strategies and tips you've read throughout this book, you'll find they pay lifelong dividends.

I have no doubt that soon people in your life will notice a remarkable change in your mindset. Your friends, loved ones, and coworkers may even be inspired by your example to develop their own mental toughness.

DID YOU ENJOY READING THE MENTAL TOUGHNESS HANDBOOK?

∼

Thank you so much for taking the time to read *The Mental Toughness Handbook*. We've come a long way, haven't we? I sincerely hope you've enjoyed the journey. It's my profound hope that the advice and exercises in this book help you to overcome any obstacle you encounter throughout your life.

www.ingramcontent.com/pod-product-compliance
Lightning Source LLC
LaVergne TN
LVHW081532060526
838200LV00048B/2066